LIBERATION

BAREFOOT DOCTOR

LIBERATION

BAREFOOT DOCTOR

THE PERFECT HOLISTIC ANTIDOTE TO
STRESS, DEPRESSION AND OTHER UNHEALTHY STATES OF MIND

Element
An Imprint of HarperCollins*Publishers*
77–85 Fulham Palace Road
Hammersmith, London W6 8JB

The Element website address is:
www.elementbooks.co.uk

and *Element* are trademarks of
HarperCollins*Publishers* Limited

Published by Element 2002

10 9 8 7 6 5 4 3 2 1

A catalogue record of this book
is available from the British Library

ISBN 0 00 714371 0

Printed and bound in Great Britain by
Scotprint, Haddington, East Lothian

Illustrations by Jane Spencer except
pgs: 82, 87, 94, 138 (top), 210 (bottom) by Senate Design Limited

Contents

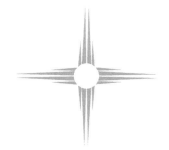

preamble text section

LIBERATION

from this being a book with no introduction

Liberation has always held romantic appeal, whether it be from slavery, poverty, hunger, war or oppression – and great liberators have always been honoured as heroes. For through liberation comes humankind's most sought-after treasure – freedom.

But as well you know, when you step on the gas and head off into the great unknown, keep driving long enough and you'll eventually run into another traffic jam, another border patrol. Now that our planet has been mostly colonized (by humans), freedom is no longer to be found by crossing external frontiers. But then, it never was – that was always an illusion.

Freedom is found within, by liberating yourself from your own internal struggle with life, in whatever form it takes, and with this comes peace. Once you've found liberation from preferring this over that, no external thing can hold you captive – not even prison walls.

If you find the key to liberating yourself from fear, greed, frustration, and other path-blocking negativities, then you unlock the prison door and walk free. In so doing, you become self-liberator and hero. Hero, because as soon as you are free, anyone privileged enough to be drawn into your personal orbit will also themselves be freed instantaneously.

Freedom is infectious — and ultimately unstoppable. It is simply a matter of being aware of the factors that entrap you from moment to moment, to different degrees at different times. It is these that prevent you fully living the unlimited life you really want, the life you can have if only you are willing to take the chance.

LIBERATION

from not knowing what to expect in this book

Well here's your chance (or at least one of them). Right now, or just a little waffle along from now, this very text is about to examine those (nasty) blocking factors and offer the relevant liberating antidotes, culled from Taoism (ancient and post-modern wayward), along with a healthy flavouring of Buddhism, Shamanism, Humanism, Positivism and Ancient Basic Commonsensism. These range from esoteric acupressure and other (arcane) physical and energetic self-healing methods and movements, to out-and-out magic, including affirmation, visualization, energy manipulation and high-intensity mental concentration, all of which have been tried and tested over the course of nearly three decades by myself and many of the tens of thousands of people I have treated or taught during that time, as well as various other assorted 'lunatics' (shout to Nico). They are conveniently simple to learn and use for anyone with half a brain (in other words, if I can get them, you certainly can).

However – and here's the disclaimer – though picked with the utmost care as methods with the widest possible universal application, with your safety and health always foremost in my mind while writing, there are many potentially powerful techniques described which, if practised inappropriately or insensitively, may cause unwanted glitches in your personal energy field that would be disruptive to your general well-being.

If suffering from any known physical or mental condition for which you may be receiving treatment, and are in any doubt, consult your alternative practitioner, family doctor, or psychiatrist before experimenting, as neither Barefoot Doctor nor, indeed, anyone involved in the production, distribution, marketing and sale of this book will be held responsible for any mishaps.

So saying, unless you're severely disconnected from your own innate intelligence and natural wisdom, you'd have to be absurdly self-destructive to derive any harm from using what's in this book. In fact, regular practice of any or all the following advice has the potential to free you of any state of mind not to your liking as and when it happens. However, as with anything worth its salt, true change occurs over time and not often all at once. So don't expect instant or near-instant changes, (though these may occur, often after you've slept on it and then come to the next day). Instead, expect to instigate a liberating process that leads to a new (entirely improved and altogether more complete, satisfying and fruitful) relationship with yourself and the world around you, a process which you can accelerate or decelerate at will, according to how actively you apply yourself to the process via the information given.

LIBERATION

from not knowing how to use this book to your optimum advantage

This book contains a slew of mind-states or blocking factors from which to liberate yourself. These have been selected from the infinite and myriad number of possible mind-states I've observed to occur with most frequency amongst the biggest number of people including of course, myself. This observation has been conducted informally over the course of two decades of healing and teaching others, three decades healing and teaching myself and, more recently, receiving an average of three hundred e-mails a day asking for advice. Though the list of mind-states included here is by no means exhaustive, I hope you'll find something to match your mood, whenever you feel at odds with yourself or reality at any given moment (assuming you have the book handy at the time).

At the head of each item will appear the title, for example, 'Liberation from Guilt', 'Liberation from Feeling like You're Always in a Rush', or even this present item's 'Liberation from Not Knowing How to Use This Book to Your Optimum Advantage' – in case you haven't been paying attention. Next, though the actual sequence of events will to some extent vary item by item (I'm not a machine and nor are you, I'm presuming), there will appear a rationalization of that blocking factor followed by an examination and diagnosis according to a melange of philosophical outlooks.

The blocking factor will be linked to its corresponding organ or organs (according to Taoist theory) and appropriate self-treatment recommended. Treatment will attend to relevant accessible trigger points, using acupressure, percussion, rubbing or energy healing, and will combine affirmations, visualizations, healing sounds, breathing patterns and (tai chi) body postures and movements to create a pleasurable and humorous moment of self-facing, self-acceptance, self-healing and, above all, self-liberation.

You will notice – if reading the book sequentially – certain descriptions of frequently used methods are repeated, often many times over. This is not to infer amnesia on your part, but to preclude the necessity of your having to memorize or study the text as such, thus keeping things as easy and effortless as can be.

I use repetition because, although the variety of mind-states you can experience in just one hour, let alone a lifetime, is infinite, all mind-states are attributable to the energetic balance of only five organs, six bowels, one brain and one set of genitals. There are only so many ways to skin a cat – ways, that is, that are universally appropriate, safe to use if used correctly, and possible to explain in a book, even as explanatory a book as this little darling.

However, rest assured that you are not being conned by not being given a new technique on every page. It is the combination of techniques used to 'treat' a particular mind-state, the order in which they are applied and the intention each time behind applying them, that counts.

I should also mention the inclusion of certain Bach Flower Remedies, but not all. This does not mean that the ones excluded are in any way invalid. I have only included the ones I've seen work time and again, both in others and myself. This is not intended as a book describing the science and art of using Edward Bach's remedies, I leave that to others more expert on the subject, but wish also to acknowledge him as one of the greatest physicians of the last millennium.

You may wish to follow all the advice relevant to removing the particular block of your choice, step by step, or you may wish to try just the bits that grab you. But do try the bits that don't grab you too – in these often lies your greater learning.

Above all, take any advice with a pinch of salt while at the same time remaining open to its possible merits and benefits. This applies to all mention of time durations in respect of techniques as these are intended only as a rough guide.

It applies even more to the actual wording of any affirmations suggested. Affirmations are your own personal tools with which to affect your internal and external realities from within and they often work best when you compose them yourself. The ones suggested are only offered to provide you with an appropriate direction to head off in relevant to the mind-state being attended to at the time, and they can be doctored at will.

4

LIBERATION

from not having a clue why Barefoot Doctor wrote this book

Though I've treated my fair share of stiff necks, bad backs, migraines, tinnitus, bowel problems and worse, all the way through to fatal diseases, my speciality has always been treating mental distress in all its forms.

Consequently, I have spent the fattest portion of over two decades 'healing' people, in other words helping them make themselves whole, helping them retrieve or preserve their sanity in the midst of personal crisis, and encouraging them to explore their full range of potential appropriate to the 'post-modern lifestyles' of today (what a sweeper that is!).

I gave up my practice two years ago now, at least I no longer charge money to heal people. I passed all my patients over to a friend who I knew would take care of them properly, and now devote all my time to spreading the knowledge (and of course, love) as broadly as possible, via all available media, in order to accelerate the process of global healing (before it's too late, personally and globally speaking).

As a result, I decided to crystallize the fruits of all that work into a book that would serve to spread the knowledge In an entertaining and straightforward enough way, so that people everywhere, no matter of which gender, age group, background culture or religion, or whether previously trained in or unaccustomed to such things or not, could benefit and have a damn good time while doing so.

For me, the decision to write a book, which, after all, isn't something you do every day, even if suffering from compulsive communication disorder as I do, begins only once I have a title. So there I was one fine day beside the sparkly blue Mediterranean sea on the Catalan coast, mind lit up by the afternoon winter sun, wondering when I should write such a book and what its title might be, when all of a sudden, like an extrater-restrial spaceship landing in the fertile fields of my imagination, came the one word I'd never used and rarely thought of, but which encapsulated the theme (if you'll excuse the grandiosity) of my life's work to date so succinctly – Liberation.

And the forests sighed and the paper mills cranked up for business ...

5

LIBERATION

from this book having no story line

So, here I sit now, almost a year later, on the 12 o'clock out of Paddington (London), one winter's day, heading west to Angel Mountain, which overlooks a rugged and magnificent portion of Welsh coastline, where (my mates) Jeb and Mike have lived on a farm self-sufficiently and organically (without being at all weird) for sixteen years now, pretty much as far into the blustery, enchanted middle of nowhere as you can get on these islands, watching patiently from magisterial heights over the stormy, sombre and definitely no-messing-about Irish Sea.

I am about to sequester myself by kind invitation, in a totally silent (other than the sound of wind and rain), hydroelectrically powered, spartanly furnished old stone barn for a round of intensive creative isolation – (to write you this book).

So if at any point the words grow dim on the page, it'll be the fluctuating voltage. On the other hand, any great uprushes of inspiration occurring randomly as you read will most likely be from power surges. It all depends on the flow of the stream whose source is a healing spring a few hundred yards away right here on Angel Mountain.

(No kidding.)

The sheer exuberance from the relief at having left London means I can hardly contain myself; liberated at last from the dubious luxury of fancy hotels, business class travel (late trains), broadband revolution and three hundred e-mails a day, meetings for plotting and planning, TV shows, quirky radio appearances, recording studios, gigs, promotional events, talks, writing copy on the run, phone calls and, of course, text messages.

I am in other words, all yours.

But are you?

All yours I mean.

Or do you live to a greater or lesser extent in reaction to others? Are you, for example (perhaps unconsciously) still attempting to please your parents, your children, your lovers, your friends, your boss, your colleagues, your teachers (and all the other children in the playground) – the perceived general public at large, in other words?

Are you a slave to other people's ideas? Or are you free?

Don't feel obliged to answer at once. Freedom's a complex issue – one where there is no clear black or white but many shades of both.

Strangely enough, and I only realized it just now, this whole writing malarkey started off for me twelve years ago, the last time I was on Angel Mountain. Friend, father figure and mentor RD Laing had just died of a heart attack playing tennis in St Tropez and Jeb (having been one of his closest friends and mine), her farm seemed the perfect place to go and cry for a few days.

In between sobbing (and laughing, as you do), during those intervals when my diaphragm was resting, I'd waft off to the barn and, by the light of an old oil light, write. (Mike hadn't yet sorted the hydroelectric at that time – it was still one of those huge future projects he'd get round to one day). I wrote for hours and hours – reams and reams of outpoured free-flow consciousness that transpired to be a personal prophecy of how my life would turn out. But the content wasn't as important as establishing a relationship between the will to write and words on page, which (surprisingly) over time developed enough that here you now sit (or stand if, say, on a crowded tube) with me about to help you liberate yourself with these very words.

(Which leads me to say), it's an amazing thing this life when you stop resisting it, when you relax your body and mind – in this particular moment, for example – let go of trying to control the results of your actions, allow things to unfold as they will and be willing to fill each moment that arises out of the nothingness with the absolute totality of yourself. Give it some welly (so to speak), before it disappears into the nothingness again.

But, most importantly, when you decide to trust this reality with all your heart, all your soul and all your mind, you notice serenely over time (because it does take time), that all you've wished for, done affirmations about, visualized and longed for all the while actually does come true.

It's a kind universe we inhabit. See that and it will be so. See it hostile and it will be. The entire quality of your experience while you're here is purely a matter of choice. Sure there's pain and suffering beyond belief. It's happening right now even while you're reading this, perhaps even in you – that's why I'm writing to you in the first place – but the more liberated you allow yourself to become, the more you'll find yourself doing to help alleviate that.

You won't help yourself or anybody else by being a miserable son of a bitch. No matter how great the pain around you: you have to remain cheerful! Not cheerful about the pain – pain hurts – but cheerful just about being alive to witness the drama of it all. Those suffering around you prefer to resonate with your joy rather than your sorrow – it makes them feel better. You could almost consider it a duty to access joy and train yourself to keep accessing it from now on, if only for the sake of good art.

True, it takes courage to be cheerful and it takes balls to be free, but you weren't 'put' on this planet whizzing round the infinite universe at 66,000 miles per hour while simultaneously rotating on its own axis at 1,000 miles per hour, to be a lily-livered slave, so courage is something well worth developing to the utmost.

I can help you reinforce that for yourself immediately, if you like. Just say, *'I have courage!'*

You think there's something funny about that? You think there's something silly about giving yourself that kind of talking to? There isn't. A good rah rah session (at least) once a day is, in fact, imperative if you wish to free yourself of the shackles of generations of pain and delusion that otherwise hinder you from full expression of self and enjoyment of life. So say it, go on,

> *'I have courage! I have courage enough to grab this adventure by the scruff of the neck, live it to the full and be cheerful no matter what, from now on!'*

I'd call you myself to acknowledge you for saying that, but now I'm here it turns out I have no signal whatsoever on my mobile (so far from 'civilization' am I), the land line phone is too many muddy footsteps away in the farmhouse and I'm simply not inclined to walk up there right now. In any case, I don't know your number and it would probably be going too far in this relationship at such an early stage of knowing you. But imagine I just have and let yourself be warmed from head to toe by the sound of it.

6

LIBERATION

from pure prose

Do you like poetry? If not, skip this and move straight to the next chapter. Otherwise, the following is offered as a lyrical template of the philosophy behind this book, which it is hoped you will enjoy immensely (the poem, the philosophy and the book).

What a pleasant adventure this.
What an elegantly poised series of discrete moments.
Ones that thrill you,
ones that fill you,
ones when it's still you,
looking out from your centre
where the madness can't enter,
while all around you the play revolves
as Shiva's endless dance evolves.

Sometimes the dance will have you squealing with fright.
Other times it'll be with delight.
You'll appear to go wrong,

you'll appear to go right,
but it's all just appearance,
a trick of the light.

You're probably wondering
how does this help me?
And I say you don't need help, you may think you do,
but as soon as you remember you're fine as you are,
all the help you need will come to you.

Now if you find that confusing
or you think I'm in some way abusing your mind,
I'll just keep it simple and say that you'll find
from this very day,
nothing will ever be the same again.
But that doesn't matter
because it never was the same before.
There are no ends, no starts,
just continuum.
Sure there are doors, but it's theatre, it's art,
and all you do is play your part.
All you do is play your part.

Let me explain:

Pleasant? Imagine attaining such a state of perpetual equipoise that you can take stock, look at this entire trip with all its gargantuan heights and unfathomable depths, then sit back and calmly indulge in such (ironic) understatement. *Adventure* because to see this gift of life otherwise, as something to be trapped and tamed in the apparent safety and predictability of mainline straight-ahead suburban cul-de-sac reality, is to deny yourself its greatest quality – *mystery*.

Only by acknowledging and surrendering to the mystery of this adventure, not knowing what comes next, does it yield up its magic and become a real-life fairy tale, wherein, against all odds, your dreams come true. (Sing *'Somewhere Over the Rainbow.'*) *Magic* because just as the 24 frames a second that make a movie appear like an unbroken stream of action, each and every moment of your own life arises of itself out of the nothingness (and everythingness) of the Tao and returns there once it's done – with your own mind being the roll of film or digital whatever upon which those still frames are stored. And this succession of independent, discrete moments is so elegantly poised, you don't even notice the joins. Well, it would be a pretty crap movie if you did.

During certain moments you'll feel thrilled to the quick just being here to witness it all. During others you'll simply feel filled and satisfied. During yet others, no matter how dramatically the action changes around you, you'll have that sense of ongoing, unchangeable identification with that still, small place or 'voice' within – the you you can't describe but who now sits here taking all this in regardless of the drama endlessly unfolding all around and within you, unfolding according to its own eternally alternating pattern of creation and destruction (Shiva's Dance, à la Hindu, or Dance of Equilibrium if you're in more of a Taoist frame of mind).

Sometimes the violence of the dance will fill you with terror and dread (mostly of making an error and winding up dead). Sometimes you'll feel nothing but pure delight.

Occasionally you'll make what look like mistakes, but which, in retrospect, turn out to be the very triggers that propel you into fresher richer pastures. Other times it will look like you're doing things right, when in fact you're walking blind into a dead-end alley. The point is, when seen from the steady inner gaze of that (in the centre) which watches (all these left turns and right and their ensuing effects), everything you experience is just passing show.

Immediately you're presented with information (like this), you wonder how it will help or enrich you (don't you?). Is there a shred of useful truth here and, if there is, how can you use it to be more enlightened and get that clear look in your eye, to be more popular, and can you market it somehow to make more money?

You (and don't think I'm singling you out here) perpetrate an illusion of being incomplete as you are and in need of completion. You think you'll be completed by acquiring something other – information, skills, wealth, possessions, status, lovers, children and friends – when in fact you are complete to begin with. It's just a game you play with yourself to give your life meaning. The paradox is that once you acknowledge yourself as being complete here and now, the world will bring you everything you want, without any effort or strain on your part and fill your life with more meaning than you know what to do with. That's what a Taoist would call *wu wei*. We in the West may call it being in a 'state of grace' and you can activate that state immediately by clicking on 'state of grace' on your internal desktop and repeating the following words up to 9 times in a row:

> *'I, (your name), am in a state of grace. I acknowledge I am*
> *complete as I am. Everything I've always wished for now*
> *begins to come true.'*

There: it's activated. But that doesn't mean you won't have to work for it, mind. You can't expect to be a lazy, slovenly, ornery bastard who never interacts and then think life will yield big results. Everything you want from the world, though originating in the Tao, will come to you through other people and it will come quicker and with a greater Impact the more you interact meaningfully with others.

Are you confused (yet)? Let me be more succinct then. You want your life to be better. Everyone does – it's part of the human condition. The desire to improve things is perhaps the major driving force of human history. So stop clinging to the past and the way things have been up to now and acknowledge that you have a choice this very moment to stop clutching and let go into the mystery in the sure knowledge that you haven't a clue what's going to happen next. However much it would appear otherwise, you can never stand in the same river twice.

But that's nothing to be afraid of, or if you are afraid, don't let that fear get in your way. From this very day, nothing will ever be the same again because everything in the world of form is in flux. But there's nothing more extraordinary about this day, hour, minute or second than any other. Every moment is an opportunity to take a different view.

A view, for example, that the dance is circular rather than in a straight line. However much it seems there are fixed end points and start points, there is just you in your centre, where the madness (of the world) can't enter, sitting still for eternity whilst the continuum of life (including your own personal round of birth, death and rebirth) unfolds from breath to breath. The changes of scenery and personnel along the way, the stage entrances and exits are merely theatrical devices, and all you need do is put yourself fully behind the role you find yourself playing from moment to moment.

I'm not saying this is true, I'm just presenting it as a view. Whether you entertain it, is entirely up to you. I don't know the 'truth' any more than you do. It just happens to be me writing the book and you reading it (this time). Always remember, you're free

21

to choose to take in whatever you like and to reject the rest – it's your book after all (unless you borrowed it).

And talking of rest, do you?

Do you ever let your thoughts come to a halt? Do you ever sit like a yew tree or even like a banana tree, empty of self and free of desire?

Take a break.

7

LIBERATION

from not knowing how your vital organs control your various states of mind

What are you feeling right now?

Does the question draw a blank?

Listen, look, feel or think into your belly. Be sensitive for a moment. Is there fear? Sadness? Excitement? Sorrow? Grief? Frustration? A combination? Nothing at all, as far as you can tell?

Does it trouble you to feel or not feel it? Does it trouble you that I ask so many questions when it's me who is meant to be coming up with the answers here?

I remember in one of my therapy phases as a younger more troubled man, paying good money for a weekly session with a most unusual therapist called Shri. We were making some progress unravelling knots when we arrived at the whole issue of feelings. When I came for the session, she had me lie down and focus on what I felt rather than what was on my mind. Fifty minutes later, I woke up to the sound of her saying, 'Well that's the end of the session.'

'But we haven't talked about anything,' I complained feeling mildly gipped.

'I told you today was about your feelings, and that's how you handle your feelings – by going unconscious on them.'

Actually, I didn't go back to her, deciding that I could quite easily go to sleep for fifty minutes on my own recognizance in future and for free, but I did get value from that last session. It made me pay attention. And now after years of practice I can tell you instantly how I feel in there. Apart from feeling damn chilly sitting in this old stone barn in the midst of a fierce Celtic coastal blizzard, to which even an entire battalion of sweatshirts layered one upon the other and the courageous antique stove in the corner are no antidote. I feel elements of fear (for being quite alone and isolated amongst all this wild, wet and blustery nature), elements of excitement for the same reasons; a mild pall of sadness for all the needless suffering in the world being caused even at this very moment through stupidity and cruelty; some grief for all the bustling activity and loved ones left behind for now; subtle frustration at not being able to think and write faster; and a distant longing for something unspecified (probably to get on a plane bound for a hot beach under a blue sky somewhere). Fear, however, is the prevalent party in the mix. And all this is subtly discernable in the precise way I am unconsciously (till now) holding the soft tissue of my belly.

I don't try to fight or change it. I simply observe and keep breathing so that the movement of breath massages the belly and prevents the feelings lodging and becoming stagnant energy, which will then make me miserable and unable to write – and seeing as there's absolutely nothing else to do around here but write, I'll be sure to avoid that little self-pity trap.

So how about you? What's going on in there? I'll just go and stand by the stove for a minute while you have a listen, look, feel or think into your own belly. While I do so, I can tell you it'll be a wonderful thing in a couple of years when Mike gets the under-floor central heating sorted out. I must say also that the wind is howling all about, it's cold, it's dark, there's no one around for miles except six mad horses in a nearby field and I'm really starting to appreciate your presence here. I hope that you're beginning to get comfortable with it and enjoy it as much as I am.

So what were you feeling? (Tell Uncle Barefoot.)

What's interesting and what will unfold through the book is how every feeling you have is related to the state of energy in your five vital organs: your kidneys, liver, heart, spleen (and pancreas complex) and lungs. The following is by no means an exhaustive explanation of the way this works in practice, and is only intended to give you a flavour of the scheme. The rest will show up over the course of the book.

Furthermore, these theories are sure to provoke harumphs and derision from more narrowly focused practitioners of Western allopathic medicine, as well as some of the more anal practitioners of Oriental medicine. If you're one of either of those and believe the following to be utter bullshit, you may well be right. However, it's bullshit that works, so try it out before drawing any final conclusions. (Thank you.)

Each of your organs and bowels along with their associated functions, correspond to one of five elements. And each organ or bowel is responsible for conducting its corresponding elemental energy through your body, mind, spirit and affairs.

Your kidneys and bladder correspond with water, liver and gall bladder with wood, heart and small intestine with fire, spleen (combined with pancreas) and stomach with earth and your lungs and large intestine with metal.

The law of the five elements states that water makes things grow (as in wood), wood burns to make fire, fire cools down to make planets (like Earth) and from the surface of planets metal can be extracted. Metal melts and becomes fluid.

So they say water feeds wood, wood feeds fire, fire feeds earth, earth feeds metal and metal feeds water.

Conversely, wood blunts metal, water puts out fire, fire melts metal, earth limits water (by forming river banks and seaside resorts, Southend-on-Sea or Acapulco to name but two), and metal, of course, cuts wood.

Everything in existence is evolving through one phase or another of these cycles. Your ability to utilize the cosmic force of yin and yang as it passes through you, doing this mad dance of five elements in a constant state of mutual feeding and checking, all depends on the relative strengths and weaknesses of your organs and bowels and the energy/chi they both produce and conduct along their respective meridians (energy or chi channels).

Moreover, your organs and bowels — each being associated with one of the five elements — determine how the dance is manifest in your body, mind and spirit and hence, by extension, how external events in your life will materialize.

For example, if your kidney chi is weak (low water), your liver will suffer (because water feeds wood). Or if your lung chi is too hot, say from smoking too much or having a hacking cough, your liver will be weakened (metal cutting wood), and if your liver energy is overheated from, say, generally being an irritable old sod, or drinking too much absinthe, your lung energy will weaken (wood blunting metal).

The whole picture – including all possibilities – is vast and endless and is probably something that can only be deeply engaged with through years of study and subsequent practice. But that doesn't stop you understanding and using the fundamental formula and applying it with great effectiveness to balance your own energy and state of emotional, spiritual, mental, physical, sexual, social and even financial health and well-being (as you'll see as you wade easily and effortlessly further along the river of lines of text that stretches out beckoningly before you).

As you move along the river, you may notice a preponderance of mind-states up for liberation that seem to be attributable either to spleen or kidneys. You may also think that's unfair for all the other organs and bowels. While every effort has been made to be fair to all innards involved, it just so happens that either the spleen, kidneys or both are at the root of most situations. Many oriental doctors believe that every problem can be treated by dealing only with the earth element (stomach and spleen), because if your connection to the planet is sound you stand a chance of being sound in all aspects. Other doctors believe everything can be treated by dealing just with the kidneys (based on the idea that as kidneys are associated with the water element and that water is such a major factor when it comes to supporting life on planets that if your kidneys are balanced, your whole life support structure has a chance of being so too).

After twenty years or more of intense clinical practice, it looks to me like both are true. Hence the preponderance. But a big shout nevertheless to your heart, lungs, and all the other bits and pieces for doing such a fine job for so long and may they all continue to do so for many years to come.

Anyway, to cut to the chase, if you feel afraid it means your kidney energy is cold and needs warming up. Conversely, if your kidneys get cold and contract it'll make you feel afraid or anxious. So, when feeling afraid, by warming your kidneys, the fear (which after all is only a form of energy) evaporates or at least stops hogging centre stage. If, on the other hand, your will is so strong no one can stand in your way no matter what and you have no friends as a result, it means your kidneys are altogether too hot and need cooling down before you go and start a war.

Your kidneys are in command of your will to survive and must be balanced for you to use it to maximum effect without damaging others as you go. They correspond to the element of water and the quality of fluidity and continuity and so generally control the flow of energy in and out of your life.

If you feel angry, frustrated or simply overbearing it means your liver is overheating – hence the word 'livid'. But when you feel depressed or shy it means your liver is cold, contracted and without sufficient blood. Your liver houses the wild one within, which needs regular channelled expression through dance, (reasonably) uninhibited socializing, exercise and meaningful interplay with the public at large in order to feel fulfilled. If this is neglected through overwork or spending too much time as an overly cultured ape, you become depressed – literally pressed down. Your liver is also in command of your personality – the socialized outward face or mask of the inner wild one (personality derives from 'persona' meaning mask in ancient Greek), and controls the degree to which you tend towards introversion or extroversion in terms of the world around you. When your liver energy is too hot and full of blood, you become bombastic and overbearing. When your liver energy is too cold and with insufficient blood you become a wallflower and a wimp.

Your liver corresponds to the element of wood, as in trees that (hopefully) grow, hence it generally controls the rate of your personal growth and development, or stagnation and entropy, as the case may be.

When you feel exhilarated, wonderful and full of joy and (hearty) laughter, no matter what the external conditions, it shows your heart energy is balanced. Happy heart, happy camper. When you feel so overly full of joy that you walk around tittering and giggling like a twit for no reason (to the extent that people think you're a bit daft), it shows your heart energy is too hot.

Your heart energy controls the tone and hue of the landscape of your mind, as well as the rate of circulation of your thoughts (just like blood), both while awake and asleep. If your mind is racing or you're suffering waking delusions of grandeur and disproportionate feelings of self-importance, or wild, crazy or unsettling dreams, it shows your heart energy is overheated. On the other hand, feeling agitated and pessimistic about everything that crosses your mind, and feeling distinctly without courage in the face of the unknown, indicates your heart energy is too cold.

Your heart corresponds to the element of fire and this lights up your eyes when they sparkle – your spirit in other words, hence it generally controls the love, warmth and passion you feel and express moment to moment.

When feeling dissatisfied, deprived, isolated, sorrowful or melancholic and you find yourself mulling over the same thing endlessly in your mind, it shows your spleen energy has gone cold and soggy and needs warming and firming up. But if you're feeling so full of your own opinions there's no room for movement, so self-satisfied you're unable to empathize with the suffering of others, so over-intellectual you can no longer feel any emotion, or so connected to the world you start believing you rule it, it indicates your spleen is too hot and dry.

Your spleen corresponds to the element of earth, the material plane, hence it generally controls your intellectual faculties and the way you get by from day to day in respect to earning your keep and the ability to monitor and maintain your personal infrastructure in good working order.

When feeling nostalgic or in any way grieving the past and hence uninspired, unimaginative and uncreative about the present, it shows your lung energy is weak and cold. If, on the other hand, you feel bored and restless where you are and keep projecting forwards into the future, especially far into the future, or are feeling too imaginative and creative to tie your shoelaces, it indicates your lung energy is overfull and overheated. When lung energy is balanced so that there is as much force behind breathing in as breathing out, you'll not be stuck in either the past or present, but firmly rooted in the 'now' (as the new age bods would say).

Your lungs correspond to the element of metal (or air) and, through their rhythmic processing of air, they generally control your overall rhythm of life.

Obviously this is an extremely crude and simplistic explanation of a highly complex equation, but unless you want this to turn into a boring old tome on Chinese medicine, it would be much better for everyone concerned to leave it at that for now. Save to say that no one feels just one thing at a time. The potential permutations of feelings and corresponding energy levels and qualities in the various organs are infinite, but will come to light later as we get into specific mind-states.

The main point is – it's actually available to you through tweaking the energy in your vital organs to regulate your state of mind continually, no matter what's going on all around you, so you reach the hallowed state of equipoise, where all you can think is 'damn this is a pleasant adventure!'

That, in turn, will liberate unprecedented amounts of hitherto snagged-up life-force (energy), which your body can then use instead to fortify your immune system and heal you of all manner of physical ailments too.

8

LIBERATION

from not knowing about energy

But what exactly is this energy, this life-force I keep so blithely referring to? It would be wiser to ask what it isn't.

Everything in this universe is energy, either active or apparently latent – (latent in the sense of being trapped in seemingly inert objects, which in fact are just examples of energy masses moving more slowly).

Energy is intelligent. (For now, accept that as an empirical observation.)

Energy is always on the move.

Energy flows relentlessly wherever it can. The more it's obstructed, the slower it flows. But like water, flow it will.

Energy flows through your body.

When you focus on energy with your mind it becomes amplified.

When energy becomes amplified you can heal with it, defend yourself with it and even do real-time magic with it, in terms of making things happen in your life or the lives of others by *wu wei*.

Wherever your mind goes your energy will follow. This is true both within your body and outside of it. If you think of your liver (under the ribs on your right, hopefully), your energy will go there now. If you think of someone (with enough intent), your energy will go to them. I say 'your energy', but in fact it's just energy. Like air, no one owns it.

Where energy goes (in your body), blood will follow and hence healing occurs.

Energy flows through your body via a series of 12 energy channels or meridians, each linked to a different organ or bowel and dealing with day-to-day environmental inter-action, as well as through a series of 8 'extra' channels which link your physical body to your 'spirit body'.

From now on, I'll probably use the word 'chi' (pronounced 'chee' as in 'cheeky' but nowadays spelt 'qi' for some unfathomable reason probably to do with Chairman Mao), instead of 'energy' or 'life-force', just because it's quicker to type, but consider all these terms interchangeable.

For now though, suffice it to say, that through unblocking the pathways of chi within your body, liberation in its widest possible sense will occur.

Talking of which ...

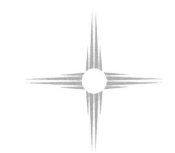

the actual liberation section

9

LIBERATION

from fear of failure

Fear of failure is wired into your circuitry from the start. It probably originates in the death cries of the billions of sperm that never make it before the lucky one that presses your particular on-button finally docks with the mother ship (egg).

Failure means different things to different people, but generally it includes being destitute, starving, drowning, suffocating, freezing or overheating to death, being unloved, disrespected, unrecognized, isolated, ostracized, unattractive, unaccomplished and undeveloped.

Fear of failure manifests in two ways: you want to run away or you indulge in over-achieving. Usually it's a combination – you work and worry yourself to the bone while simultaneously harbouring a variety of escape fantasies. Hence the pattern of slogging it out all week long and getting pissed or stoned on a Friday night, working week in week out and running off for a two-week holiday in the sun once, twice or even thrice a year, or slaving away your prime to be able to afford a decent retirement. However, that's all fine and normal. You can go along for years in a state of constant low-grade anxiety, sabotaging yourself more or less subtly here and there in this way and that, sustaining a mild chronic workaholic condition, daydreaming of desert islands, driving yourself like a bit of a demon who's drank too many espressos, watching too much TV and occasionally going off on punishing adventure treks through the Andes or the odd 10-day vipassana meditation retreat. But eventually your life becomes unbalanced in one direction or another, begins causing you undue stress, makes you ill or mad and all of a sudden you think 'what a silly boy (or girl) I am'.

There is absolutely no point fighting this fear of failure. That would be like fighting with your own leg. It would just hurt and hamper you, waste precious energy and leave you even more prone to and afraid of failure than before.

Liberation from this fear will only be found by first accepting it, then welcoming it for what benefits it confers, and finally reabsorbing it in its raw energetic form into your kidneys whence it originally sprang (as springs all fear), and where it can be transformed in a trice into positive energy to fuel your success.

To instigate this process, your mind has to be brought fully into play, by commanding it along the following lines (and this is only intended as a guide, so substitute your own phraseology at will)

> *'I am now willing to accept this fear of failure, to welcome it for the benefits it confers (such as getting me out of bed in the morning), to reabsorb it energetically and to transform it into its opposite form: courage and confidence in success – the will to succeed.'*

Before going further it is necessary to anchor this command to the physical world of fact by that most fundamental of all voluntary actions – breathing and, specifically, exhalation. Exhalation is the most immediate act of release you can perform – release being crucial to the mechanics of liberation – expelling as it does the stale air (environment) of the past from your lungs and along with it, any negative energy you wish to be relieved of.

Start by expelling (fully) all the old air from your lungs, imagining it carrying with it all negative energy associated with the fear of failure. Now, as the new air rushes in to fill your lungs, imagine it to contain the antidote – the will to succeed. Consciously repeat this idea-impregnated breath cycle at least 9 times or until you are part- mesmerized by it, so that it continues automatically like a sub-refrain through the practice contained in this liberation and beyond.

As with food, acceptance of information occurs physically In your upper abdomen. Look, listen, feel or think into your upper abdomen, your solar plexus, the repository where all feelings including fear are experienced, and allow yourself to recognize this particular fear of failure as a physical sensation. Don't squirm away from it. Just feel it. Don't try to mask or change it. Just be with it and continue to breathe (it) – out with the fear, in with the antidote.

Once you have it fully in frame and you're all squared off to it, adopt the polite approach and thank it for all the benefits it confers – mostly the impetus to succeed – and say, 'Fear-Of-Failure – thank you.' Then tell it, while it's off its guard and still chuffed with itself for being thus praised by its host,

'I no longer require you to play such a prominent role on my internal stage – you are henceforth being honourably retired to the wings. Will-To-Succeed will be taking over your role from now on.'

Fear-Of-Failure will be sad, of course, even mildly put out. But you're the director around here and what you say goes. Let it be sad and let the sadness pass through you like a wave and be done with.

Fear of no matter what, but especially fear of failure, illness (another form of failure) and death (the ultimate failure when seen from this pessimistic perspective), arises of itself whenever your kidney energy is low. This deficit may be hereditary, may be due to chronic anxiety and nervousness (also possibly hereditary), may be from a sustained period of life-stress or even just from physical cold and damp. Any or all of these will cause the area around your kidneys to contract, thus constricting blood and chi flow and producing an ongoing uprush of fearful chi and subsequent discomfort and unease in your upper abdomen – in this case, fear of failure, probably due to unconscious fear of body (kidney) failure.

Conversely, by physically and energetically inducing this constriction to ease and thus increase circulation through the kidneys, the fearful chi will be dispersed and automatically replaced by its antidote – the will to succeed, which is what arises of itself whenever your kidneys are correctly energetically balanced and physically relaxed.

To effect this now, place the backs of your fists against the soft part of your lower back, one either side of your spine, knuckles pointing downwards, and rub briskly up and down a few inches in either direction, to generate immense heat in your kidney region. Once felt, stay your hands, letting them rest over your kidneys till the heat penetrates. And as it does, visualize the entire region relaxing and releasing itself from constriction.

Meanwhile, continue breathing out your fear and breathing in your will to succeed, but now see this occurring around and within the kidneys themselves. So that each exhalation is felt to expel the fear of failure from your kidneys and each inhalation to draw the will to succeed into them.

Finally, ignite the effect by using your finger to press firmly into the dead centre of your breastbone to spark up courage from your heart to throw in the mix, and as you do so, declare proudly yet modestly,

'Now I am willing to succeed, in fact I'm willing to be so successful, I'll probably want to eat myself.'

Practise this entire procedure faithfully 3 nights in a row, immediately and whenever you feel the fear coming back, and within no more than 50 or 60 years you'll never be afraid of failing again.

10

LIBERATION

from self-pity

Self-pity is insidious. It creeps up from behind and takes you in a stranglehold before you realize and starts sapping your chi. Nor is it something you triumph over once and for all. Like dealing with weeds in a herb garden, you keep having to root it out.

And every time you turn your back on it, it jumps up and grabs you again.

It has nothing much to do with your environment or circumstances either. You can be having the best of times in the most salubrious of places and are just as prone to attack as when having the worst of times in the grottiest of places.

You can always tell when it's got you though. First, you notice you're not having a good time. Then you want to be somewhere else, usually with someone else (other than who you're with), doing something different (or differently), and then your body becomes tense from resisting what's happening.

Now you may be reading this in prison, in hospital, homeless in a doorway (or even without a doorway) or you may be working under contract in a job you hate or embroiled in a relationship you can't abide, and consider yourself perfectly justified in feeling sorry for yourself. But do you gain anything by it? I mean, I know there's nothing like a good moan, even when there's no one there to listen, but all you achieve by wallowing in it, as opposed to liberating yourself from it, is to diminish your experience of life in the moment and to limit your range of possibilities.

I'm personally having a round or two with it myself right now, battling with a dead fire and wet tinder, warding off the all-pervasive cold and damp sweeping incessantly down from the stern hills behind the barn, and missing contact with the outside world, apart from you, that is. It comes over in waves and can be triggered by the slightest thing, like the fire going out in the stove, which will demoralize me for a good forty seconds or so until I pull myself together – I take it personally, as if the stove doesn't like me and is doing it on purpose.

Self-pity disguises itself like a computer virus, an e-mail with an attachment detailing a thousand plausible reasons why I should return to the city with its adequate mobile phone coverage, central heating and warm, dry, clean-sheeted beds.

But I notice that when I overcome it like a big, brave boy, say by marching over to the stove with focused intent and spending twenty minutes stoking up a respectable blaze (I'm such a city boy at heart) when I'd rather be working or spending an hour or so in the drizzle and sleet outside doing tai chi, making peace with the magnificence of my surroundings, then my sense of self-respect grows and I'm happy to postpone my escape plans till later.

(Don't worry that all this liberal insertion of (my)self into these pages of yours might be turning this into one of those awful California-style self-help books, where the author recounts tale after dreary tale of their boring, goody-two-shoes new age lives until you just want to throw the book away or give it to me to use for tinder. It's not, I promise.)

The first thing you have to do in order to liberate yourself from self-pity is notice it happening.

The next thing is to not to get all silly and say, *'Self-Pity, fuck off, you're an out-and-out drag!'* because that will make it angry and it's a lot cleverer and more powerful than you think. Instead be gracious. Sidestep and declare with hand on heart, *'It's perfectly fine and OK for me to entertain this self-pity as long as I find it enjoyable.'*

That'll both confuse the dickens out of Self-Pity and remind you that you're the one in charge here and you have a choice. Obviously there's nothing gained by not enjoying being here, however nasty things seem. Neither is anything gained by wishing to be somewhere else if the road isn't yet ready to receive you (nor by wishing to be with someone else if you can't even get a signal on your mobile phone so you can call and invite them). So the quicker you choose to liberate yourself from self-pity the better for everyone concerned, including Self-Pity, who is then free to go wherever it is more welcome.

Self-pity, as in any sense of lack or deprivation in the moment, though possibly (apparently) triggered by circumstances, in fact arises from weakness of the spleen. Your spleen chi is responsible for ensuring you feel adequately fed. Not just with food, but with life in general. Hence, when your spleen is of sound adjustment you feel satisfied no matter how unsatisfactory your circumstances and when it is maladjusted you feel dissatisfied even in a warm, clean, well-appointed luxury hotel room.

To stimulate your spleen chi into a state of balance, begin by pressing the fingertips of your right hand in under the ribs on the left hand side of your abdomen. Use your left hand to add weight to your right and push in till you feel slightly winded. Maintain the pressure while breathing fluidly, deeply and slowly, relaxing your entire body as much as you can. Keep pressing till you really want to stop and then release the pressure slowly and gradually, returning your hands to whichever position they were in before, holding this book, probably, or something totally different.

Next, find that sideways protruding hump on the inside of your foot, at the base of the big toe – where people get bunions. Press into it where the soft flesh meets the hard, at the end nearer to you, with either a small improvized kneading tool (such as a pen top) or with thumb, fishing around for the most sensitive spot and focusing the pressure on it for a moment or three. This is the source point on the spleen meridian, daily pressure on which will encourage your spleen to draw in more energy from its elemental source, the earth beneath your feet.

Spleen 3

Finally, stand with the soles of your feet (barefooted or shod) firmly planted on the floor, toes spread as wide as you can muster and visualize thousands of roots growing down from your soles towards the Earth's centre, and with this image clear in your mind (and feet) say,

'I am king (or queen) of no matter what!'

11

LIBERATION

from inertia

Sometimes you're a smooth boulder, rolling frictionless down the mountainside, at other times you're a jagged rock jammed into a crag and unable to move an inch. Obviously, everyone wants to be a boulder because it's more fun, but sometimes you just get stuck where you are, unable to motivate yourself to do even the smallest thing.

It all starts in your mind. Your thoughts lose their fluidity and become rough and spiky, square and obtuse and get stuck in crevices in the recesses of your mind. Where your thought goes, your energy follows and soon your energy flow backs up and you come to a standstill, pretty much like a crowded rush-hour tube (metro or subway train) stuck in a tunnel because there are three trains in the tunnel in front of you.

As everything alive moves and everything that isn't doesn't, it's safe to say that movement is good for your health. Movement not just through time and space, but also movement or progress in personal growth, creative pursuits, personal relationships and business projects or career trajectories.

As soon as you stop developing yourself in any area, stagnation occurs. This leads to entropy which affects all aspects of self. So, if you find yourself inert for any length of time when you could be more advantageously engaged in activity of some sort, and it's troubling you (or your bank manager), immediately focus on whatever is moving inside you – for what you focus on grows.

Your heart is beating and your blood is circulating. Your diaphragm is moving up and down as you breathe in and out. Your stomach is processing food. Your intestines are sorting and sifting and producing waste. Your kidneys are doing likewise with fluids. Your liver is purifying your blood. Your glands are secreting and even your eyeballs are moving from side to side as you read the lines in this book. So you're not really inert at all – quite 'ert' in fact. And as you allow yourself awareness of what's moving within you, that movement becomes amplified until you want to get up and do something.

But don't just yet.

Stay where you are and breathe slowly, evenly and fluidly. With shoulders totally relaxed, without any effort or strain, holding the book in your left hand, slowly raise your right arm, elbow slightly bent and hand open, until straight out in front of you at chest height with your palm facing the left. Now, as if moving your hand through water instead of air, soften all the muscles of your arm and wave it slowly and sensitively from right to left and left to right in front of you at chest height no more than 9 times. Transfer the book into your right hand now and wave with the left the same amount of repetitions.

If you noticed a pleasant sensation of fullness in your palms while making the passes, that'll be chi. Enjoy the sensation of release in the shoulder and along the arm as you slowly lower each hand. And as you settle back into regular two hand book-reading mode, remind yourself, *'I am able to access the power to move at will.'*

That inside you which wants to move, the raw impulse of the wild and untamed, is said to 'live' in your liver. Your liver chi, in other words, that which urges you to live life (hence liver), is responsible for motivation. When held fast by inertia, your liver chi stagnates. By reinstating the flow, inertia will dissolve of itself.

Observing the top of your unshod foot, notice how the bone of your big toe joins the large bone of the foot and the bone of the next toe along does likewise. In the depression formed between where the bones meet is the source point of your liver meridian. Using a small improvised poking instrument such as the blunt end of a knitting needle or a fingertip, press firmly into the depression until you feel a mild ache. Keep pressing for a few moments, release and repeat on the other foot.

Liver 3

This will encourage your liver to draw more chi from its elemental source, wood – that which grows, or nature – and help set up the right environment for the motivation to grow.

At a muscular level, it is said (by practitioners of tai chi and other martial arts practised with deeply bent knees) that motivation originates in the muscles in the front of your thighs, your quadriceps. By stimulating blood and chi flow in the quadriceps, you activate motivation.

(Holding the book between your teeth – kidding – or placing it on a nearby supportive surface), curl up your hands into fists and using the surface formed at the edge of your little finger, drum a steady roll of beats lasting a minute or so up and down the top of your thighs, one fist to each thigh.

As the beats die out and your hands return to normal book-reading position, while enjoying the sensation of blood and chi circulating in your thighs, declare,

'Now I'm so motivated I could eat myself!'

12

LIBERATION

from loneliness

Loneliness is a choice you make. You can sit on a mountain for days on your own without feeling lonely. You may feel bored or confused about why you're sitting on a mountain, but you don't necessarily feel lonely.

You can be at home with your loved ones and feel lonely. Loneliness is not the same thing as being alone.

Loneliness arises when you lose your sense of connectedness with the world around you and the six billion people with you on the planet as you read this.

Loneliness originates in losing your conscious connection with your own spirit, your guardian angel, your god, your higher, bigger self, or however you think of the ineffable consciousness that connects, informs and animates us all – the Tao. This happens when there is insufficient chi flowing through your chest and then the musculature involved with your breastbone subtly contracts in an attempt to armour you from feeling the pain of isolation.

What you need is a good, fat hug, a total breastbone-to-breastbone affair, to soften up your chest and inject some human warmth into you. I'd hug you myself but I'm busy right now, so, if at all possible, find someone trustworthy and warm and give them a hug. If this is impractical owing to your being geographically isolated or standing on a crowded train with total strangers, you'll have to do it yourself.

In the manner of someone crossing their arms, grip the book between your teeth – kidding again – or set it down on a convenient surface, give yourself a deep hug and say, *'I'm all right, I'm all right.'* Next, taking the book in your left hand, place your right palm firmly on the centre of your chest. Move your hand slowly in clockwise circles so the muscles of your chest turn with it over the breastbone, 9 times, and with each circle repeat one word in turn from the statement:

'I ... am ... always ... exactly ... where ... I'm ... meant ... to ... be.'

The energy you activate in your chest like this is known as your heart protector chi and, paradoxically, it only circulates when you are relaxed and not trying to emotionally protect yourself. In other words, to be truly energetically protected so you don't feel the pain of isolation, you have to be vulnerable.

To allow this vulnerability requires courage, also a property of heart protector chi, hence the word courage which derives from the French word coeur, meaning heart. Courage to be vulnerable can be activated by pressing between the two tendons that run up the middle of the inside of your forearm from the centre of the underside of your wrist into the crook of your elbow, approximately 2 inches up from that faint band of interwoven lines that form a bracelet on the underside of your wrist.

Press with your thumb firmly enough to make the point ache and make your hand feel paralyzed and hold for about a minute, repeating on the other arm immediately afterwards.

Heart Protector 6

Now tell me, during that whole procedure did you actually feel lonely for a minute?

Visualize yourself now connected from the centre of your chest by tendrils of invisible light to (the centre of the chests of) all like-minded people on the planet, people who are or could be your friends, in whose company you'd not feel lonely, including actual or potential lovers.

Imagine yourself sending chi along all the tendrils at once, like doing a mass e-mail, watching as all the like-minded people on the planet light up one by one with a bing and that little voice saying, 'you have mail'. Then call out (internally) as if you have the attention of every one of them and say,

'People of like mind, I'm ready to connect with you in time and space! Let's do it before I go nuts!'

Then wait but a few days, (or longer if geographically isolated without reasonable expectation of meeting any humans in the vicinity, say if you're out at one of the poles or wherever) and without even trying or making any effort at all, you'll find yourself beginning to make meaningful contact with kindly souls once again and loneliness will evaporate.

13

LIBERATION

from doubt

Doubt – not feeling steady on the water, not trusting where the river's taking you, not trusting yourself – is fine if you enjoy that kind of thing. Trusting yourself is more fun though.

When you doubt yourself, you leak chi from your kidneys and this attenuates your immune response and opens you up all to kinds of physical or psychical weaknesses. When you trust yourself, your kidneys relax, you stop peeing so much, your sex drive increases and your immune response improves. By strengthening your kidney chi, specifically by warming it up, you feel less doubtful and more sure of yourself.

We're talking about confidence, literally holding faith with yourself. This implies the necessity for some kind of inner dialogue between that within which calls the shots and that which doubts.

Cast your mind back to the moment your father's sperm implanted itself successfully in your mother's egg and you, through the exponential multiplication of cells, grew against all the odds to full term and managed, by hook or by crook, to make it through to the outside world. From here you underwent the rigours of learning to feed, digest and eliminate, the emotional minefield of the family hearth, the psychological disturbance of kindergarten and school, the shock of entering the marketplace to rent out your working hours, and so on till this point of reading these words.

Immediately acknowledge yourself for having made it thus far and consider the unbroken internal thread of you-ness that watched all that theatre as it unfolded before your eyes and around your quaking boots. And as that one who watches, say to the one who doubts, as one desperado to another, '*I got us this far, didn't I? Now trust me to get us where we're meant to be going (wherever that is), and get us there safely!*' Or you could just look the one who doubts square in the eye and say, '*Shuddupa your face!*' Either way, the democratic or the dictatorial, you have to take command now.

Start by settling and warming your kidneys. Gripping the book between your teeth, or setting it down on a convenient surface, take a hot water bottle and apply it to your lower back in an alternating on–off motion no more than 36 times. Then, setting the hot water bottle down, use the backs of your hands to rub briskly over the same area in an up-and-down motion 3 inches or so either way, until your kidneys feel warmed to the core.

Now, with your feet 1 foot or so apart and both facing forward as if standing astride the rails of a very narrow gauge railway track, slowly hang forward from the waist without straining your lower or upper back, until you feel a stretch in the backs of your legs. Relax into the position, focusing on allowing your backbone to elongate, enjoying the stretch in your hamstrings and warmth and openness in your kidneys and say, *'I surrender!'*

Straighten yourself slowly starting at the hips with your head coming up last until standing upright, then start repeating like a train running down those tracks,

'I trust myself, I trust myself, I trust myself, I trust myself, I trust myself, I trust myself, I trust myself, I trust myself, I trust myself, I trust myself, I trust myself, I trust myself.'

And keep repeating it for no more than 3 days solid, by which time you'll be so confident you'll be looking for mountains (to move).

And if you doubt that, simply go back to the top of the item and read it again.

14

LIBERATION

from shyness at social functions

You walk into a party where you know hardly anyone or no one at all and you feel painfully shy. Don't try and change it. Be shy. It's fetching if carried with dignity, vulnerability and authenticity.

Shyness, when you look at it, is irrational fear of being rejected or humiliated by people you don't even know.

Fear in general occurs when your kidney chi is cold and weak. Shyness in particular arises when your liver chi overheats and evaporates the (liver) blood, which controls the strength and presence of your personality. The liver chi overheats and evaporates the blood in your liver when your kidney chi grows cold through contraction either from a period of illness, generally stressful lifestyle, cold, damp climate, pre-menstrual syndrome, chronic low-grade anxiety or fear, overuse of 'recreational' drugs, coffee or alcohol, or a combination of all of the above (with the exception of PMS if you're a boy).

This is because your kidneys, corresponding to the water element, are responsible for maintaining the liver (wood) at a cool enough temperature not to catch light from the fire of the heart and evaporate the blood it stores and purifies. (Bear in mind that this is according to Oriental medical philosophy, not Western, and is a highly poetic way of describing energetic functions.)

The safest way to cool your liver is to drink at least 5 strong cups of tea made from dried chrysanthemum flowers (obtainable from any Chinese supermarket or herbalist, but use dried flowers rather than the teabags which have loads of added sugar). The quickest way to boost liver blood levels is to eat a beetroot every day before lunch, especially on those days when you have a social do to attend later on.

To warm your kidney chi, eat a small knob of raw ginger or drink a strong cup of ginger tea every day in the late afternoon, especially in the cold of winter.

Three times a day, press with thumbs directly behind your inner ankles, between ankle bone and Achilles tendon until you feel a sharp ache. This stimulates the source point on your kidney meridian and will encourage your kidneys to draw more chi from their element of water or moisture in the air. Maintain pressure for a minute or so, then release and rub the backs of your hands briskly and firmly on your lower back, one hand each side of the spine, in an up-and-down motion 3 inches or so in each direction for a minute or two.

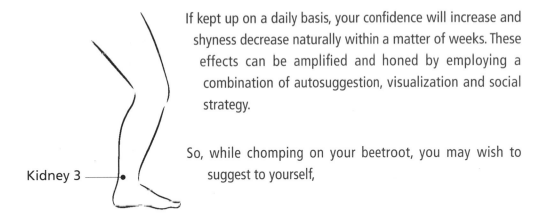

If kept up on a daily basis, your confidence will increase and shyness decrease naturally within a matter of weeks. These effects can be amplified and honed by employing a combination of autosuggestion, visualization and social strategy.

So, while chomping on your beetroot, you may wish to suggest to yourself,

'I now choose to find myself highly entertaining and pleasing in the company of others, especially those I've never met before.'

Or simply,

'I am highly pleasing in the company of others, whether I've met them before or not.'

And while quaffing your chrysanthemum brew, you may wish to visualize yourself with a powerful magnet in your chest drawing people to you without you having to expend any energy whatsoever. See yourself at a social do surrounded by people who just want to be near you, to hear you speak and perhaps touch the hem of your garment if given the chance. See yourself, in other words, interacting easily, confidently and fluently with interesting strangers and in time you'll find it happening in real-time of itself. (For as you see it, so shall it be.)

And for a workable, effective strategy in four parts, specifically for stand-up and chat events of any kind, with or without dancing, try this:

On entering the venue look everyone you pass by or are introduced to in the eye and smile warmly, where appropriate. If you find yourself standing awkwardly on your own not knowing which way to look, scan the venue and find the most comfortable looking place to sit, preferably in the hub of the activity. In time, as they start getting fed-up standing around or dancing, people, especially those you've managed to make eye contact with, will be drawn to you, if only in the hope they'll be able to steal your seat when you go to the toilet. In fact, they'll be unconsciously responding to the welcoming vibrations in your energy field set up by having regularly visualized that magnet in your chest.

Once someone is drawn into your orbit, you may be obliged to either instigate or maintain a conversation. If stuck for words, instead of succumbing to talking a load of shit, maintain eye contact and ask simple questions regarding such basic, fundamental issues as birth sign, age, where they grew up, what their parents were like during the growing-up period, how they earn a living, what their life's ambition is (if any), how old they are and what fascinates them most in the world. As they talk, look out for any apparent positive qualities and take a chance of acknowledging them for those. Obviously, you can only pull this off if genuinely interested in them at the time, otherwise you'll just come across as desperate and false. Basically, people will be interested in you if you're interested in them.

Be assured that most people feel shy at social events, especially when they don't know anyone, which is why so much alcohol (and cocaine) is consumed as social lubricant. You're not a freak because you feel shy. People are as scared of you as you are of them, however with-it, confident and in-the-know they seem to be. Realizing this will help you see beyond masks and have compassion for the human condition, including your own, which lies beneath.

And now a little ditty. Repeat after me,

'It's perfectly OK for me to feel shy,
I can still be a popular girl (or guy).'

15

LIBERATION

from indecision

Strangely enough, I'm finding it hard to decide how to start this item. If only I could read it first, I'd know which way to go. But then I notice it's already begun writing itself regardless and all I have to do is follow it and see what happens.

Which in effect, is exactly how to liberate yourself from indecision.

Looking back over things, you could say it was predestined, but no one alive has ever known for sure whether there really is such a thing as destiny, other than when looking at things with hindsight. No one even knows whether free will actually exists. The greatest philosophers have spent (or wasted, depending on how you look at it) years pondering this issue without drawing any meaningful conclusions.

You could just say that the Tao, the great way of all things, simply has a habit of making things happen as they will, according to a chain of cause and effect with its roots in an infinite past.

You'd still be none the wiser.

According to the principles of tai chi boxing, when an opponent attempts to strike your right side, rather than resist and block the strike, you yield to it by turning your body at the waist further to the right. Your right side being thus empty, your opponent's strike finds nothing to connect with and its force is spent. Meanwhile, this turning at the waist to the right has caused your left arm to swing round of itself and strike your opponent on their right side, pretty much with the same amount of force as in their original attempted strike at you. By being empty yet grounded and centred, you have deflected their force and sent it back to strike them.

This, however, requires great courage. If you yield a nanosecond too soon, your opponent will spot it and land the punch regardless. So you have to wait until the very last moment after their striking action has already been set in motion before responding by turning at the waist.

It is like being targeted by a heat-seeking missile (not that I ever have been). You'd have to wait until the very last moment before running (extremely) quickly to one side, so that the missile would slam into the wall behind you instead and explode. If you moved too soon, it would simply follow and find you. True, it wouldn't be a pretty picture for you either way, but it serves to illustrate a point. That is, if you empty yourself and allow the force of events to build sufficiently to start pushing up against your chest, waiting courageously until the very last moment before responding by turning this way or that, there'll be no actual choice to make. You will, in other words, have used the oncoming force of events to propel you forwards on your path.

Everything you need to know is revealed precisely when you need to know it and not a moment before (or after). The state of indecision only arises when, not accessing the courage to wait for the force of events to have built up sufficiently to work with, you engage in a futile, energy-wasting attempt to outguess it.

But as well as requiring courage, responding to life like this requires you be alert, perceptive to the slightest changes and ready for instantaneous action at all times. It also requires you remain centred, balanced and rooted enough to yield to the oncoming force of events without being toppled and flattened.

It's a dance. But not one you do lying down (except for when resting, sleeping, having a massage or another form of treatment, engaging in various sexual activities or performing certain yogic manoeuvres) – you have to stay on your feet.

So in the midst of driving yourself mad trying to decide what to do, stop, drop your mind down into your belly, specifically where your small intestine lives, and wait.

Just as your small intestine sorts what is good for you to retain and what is better to eliminate as waste, in respect of the food you eat, it also 'decides' what is good for you and what is not, which way to adopt and which way to leave behind, in respect of life in general. (I love that phrase, 'life in general'. Three words that can mean so much and so little simultaneously. But I digress. Mind you, there's nothing wrong with a bit of idle chit chat while you're waiting for your small intestine to reveal which way to go next).

In other words, you'll know exactly what to do next because you'll literally feel it in your guts.

To accentuate this function over time so that you respond effectively to all incoming information and thus make the best decision every time, hold the book in your left hand and use the fingertips of your right hand to press gently but firmly into the centre of your belly, approximately 1 inch above your navel. Being sure not to hold your breath, maintain pressure at a comfortable but stimulating level for no longer than 50 seconds or so and release slowly, affirming as you do,

'I am alert, perceptive to the slightest change of external conditions and ready for instantaneous response. Everything I need to know will be revealed.'

Everything you need to know will be revealed. Until then, relax, let go, allow life to happen and enjoy yourself.

16

LIBERATION

from feeling guilty

I doubt there's a person alive, on this planet at least, who for whatever reason isn't guilty of having at some point wilfully violated the well-being of themselves or someone else, whether human or otherwise.

Flick your awareness back over the thing or things you have done to violate yourself or others during your life so far.

You are guilty of these transgressions.

Accept it, say, 'I am guilty of this', and let it go. Let it go, because you have no obligation to make yourself suffer for it. Enough suffering was caused at the time without needing to keep on adding to it. Whoever you may have hurt, including yourself, will receive no real benefit from your suffering.

This isn't an ideal world, however hard we strive to make it so. Creatures violate each other – it's part of nature's dynamic. Sometimes it's you that does it. Sometimes it's you it's done to.

This isn't to suggest you should go into denial about the significance of the pain you may have caused. Far from it. It's to suggest you hold awareness of the fact, simply as a fact, without attaching a rider clause that says you have to suffer over it. You just say, 'Yes I am guilty', and get on with it.

After all, you don't learn to be a kind person by being unkind to yourself (walking around feeling guilty all day). You learn to be kind simply by consciously practising being kind – both to yourself and others. And this is true no matter how cruel or twisted you may have been in the past.

By simply watching yourself with compassion, judging the merits and demerits of your actions as you go along, but without passing sentence, you become far more conscious of the significance of what you're doing moment to moment and so far less likely wilfully to hurt yourself or others again.

People say guilt sucks, but it's not guilt that sucks. Guilt is just guilt – a statement of your accountability, if you like. What sucks is indulging in the shame and self-flagellation that you've chosen to attach to the guilt. It literally sucks the chi out of you, leaving you weakened and less able to contribute to the world in a meaningful way from then on.

It is probable that guilt is merely disguised fear of retribution either divine or by the person wronged, which is why you punish yourself with shame and self-flagellation. It's a way, thinks your unconscious mind, to make amends so you don't get punished. Which is patently absurd.

Nonetheless, shame arises when your spleen chi is weak. Conversely, when you feel shame, it weakens your spleen chi. Spleen chi is in charge of accepting and assimilating food into your system. This includes food for thought as well as your belly. When spleen chi is deficient, not only will you have a hard time digesting your dinner, you'll also have a hard time digesting who you are – you'll find it difficult to accept yourself.

Meanwhile the self-flagellatory urge arises from your liver overheating as an expression of inwardly turned anger. Your spleen and liver have a reciprocal see-saw energetic relationship. The liver tends to be the greedier of the two, while the spleen tends to keep itself to itself. So whenever your spleen energy weakens, in this instance because of feeling shame over something you're guilty of having done, it is susceptible to being invaded by the greedy liver and having its chi hijacked. If this happens, your liver will overheat due to the excess chi it is now carrying, and will find expression in inwardly turned anger, hence self-flagellation. If a person in this condition is without self-awareness, say in the case of a psychopath, the anger will be turned outwards instead (which is why violent criminals or warmongers tend towards a compulsion to repeat their crimes).

To liberate yourself from the shame of guilt and thereby initiate a lifelong process of making amends by being kind to yourself and others from now on, start by performing the following.

Setting the book down on a convenient surface, place your left palm on your left side in line with the lower ribs and your right palm just to the right of that. Draw first your right hand and then the left across your upper abdomen as far to the right as they'll go, in alternating strokes, no more than 180 times. When done, rest your palms with your right one on your right side in line with the lower ribs and the left one just to the left of that, in a mirror image of the starting position, and let the heat penetrate to your liver. This tricks your liver by giving it what it wants without a fight – the chi from your spleen – and lulls it into a false sense of security.

After a few moments, with your palms resting there, repeat the stroking business in reverse, from right to left, being sure to count the same number of strokes but no more than 180. When finished, rest your hands at the original starting position and allow the heat to penetrate to your spleen.

Not only does this encourage self-acceptance. If performed on a daily basis, it also helps to strengthen your digestive system (helping to prevent bloating, flatulence, indigestion and irritable bowel), boost immune response, tonify your diaphragm and hence your lungs, and give your upper arms a bit of gentle exercise.

Now, imagining you have a hole or breathing aperture in your solar plexus (centre of upper abdomen), start to breathe in and out through it. As you do, visualize every out-breath carrying away all residue of shame and self-flagellatory tendencies and every in-breath flooding the region with the essence of self-acceptance.

When you've done no more than 9 breath cycles like this, stop, raise your face skywards and proclaim,

'I am absolved!'

As well as taking pine Bach Flower remedy whenever suffering a particularly strong bout of the guilties, make this procedure part of your daily experience.

In no time at all, you'll be feeling so guilt-free you'll be applying to the Pope for canonization.

17

LIBERATION

from cynicism

While cynicism in measured doses has its place in informing and lending a slight edge to your repertoire, (indeed without it most of us would be insufferable wide-eyed, gung ho bores), it is, like cocaine, a dangerous drug. Its effects on your personality can be noticeable but relatively subtle, yet its effects on your soul and, ultimately, your health in general can be relatively severe. Cynics are merely disappointed idealists and tend to be extremely sensitive souls in disguise.

Cynicism is an armouring device you employ to protect yourself from being hurt (again) by a world full of people and events that didn't quite live up to your (once unrealistic) expectations. You employ it both to mask your fear of being hurt again and to express a little of your suppressed original anger over the initial disappointment.

Like cocaine, cynicism adversely affects the energy circulating in your chest, known as your heart protector chi, by inhibiting its flow, and thus causing the musculature and connective tissue of your chest to harden, in order to deaden the pain. However, by closing down the chi in your chest, you limit your capacity to ever feel exuberant again.

It may well now be time to forgive life. Forgive your mother, your father, your siblings, your nanny, your grandparents, your teachers, your heroes, your friends, your partners, your colleagues and the man and woman in the street. Forgive the sun, the moon, the stars, the Earth, nature and infinite space. Forgive the priests, the playwrights, the politicians, the gangsters and the whores. Forgive the ones who go up two semitones at the end of each sentence or phrase. Forgive the weather. Forgive destiny. Forgive your god. Even forgive people who wear brown shoes with navy trousers, but above all, forgive yourself – for being such a cynical bastard all these years. It's time to move on.

I don't mean you can regress to a state of false naivety and unrealistic expectations, but you can move on in full knowledge and acceptance of the nastiness, brutality and cruelty inherent in life. And yet move on in full expectation of the grandeur, elegance and benevolence also inherent in it, for what you focus on grows.

You may have been hurt in the past – it would be a rare person who hasn't, but don't waste any more energy vainly trying to protect yourself from pain in the future. Of course, you'll feel pain again (how could you expect not to?), but pain only hurts while you resist it. As soon as you accept it, relax into it and choose to use it as fertiliser for your personal growth instead, it ceases to hurt, becomes merely a sensation, then disappears.

With the surface formed at the end of each fist by the edge of your curled palm and little finger, start the decynicizing process this instant by percussing Tarzan-like, a swift and steady drum roll on the centre of your breastbone for no more than 90 seconds, while simultaneously chanting the sound 'Haaaaaaaaah!' in as deep and resonant a tone as you can comfortably muster for the duration. Towards the end of the role, slow the tempo gradually and progressively until your fists come to rest of themselves.

This will help dislodge your armour and reinstate the flow of heart protector chi, which you will notice as a tingling sensation in the chest as your drum roll and *'haaaaaaaaahing'* end and silence fills the valleys once again.

Then with arms stretched out to the sides crucifix-style (to stretch open the arm meridians of heart and heart protector), take an extremely full, deep breath and say,

'I forgive my mother, father, siblings [where applicable], nanny [or other carers], grandparents, teachers, heroes, friends, partners, colleagues and the man and woman in the street.

'I forgive the sun, the moon, the stars, the Earth, nature and infinite space. I forgive the priests, the playwrights, the politicians, the gangsters and the whores.

'I forgive the ones who go up two semitones at the end of each sentence or phrase.

'I forgive the weather, destiny and my god.

'I even forgive people who wear brown shoes with navy trousers, but above all, I forgive myself – for being such a cynical bastard all these years. It's time to move on.'

Then relax your arms and carry on as you were and results should start showing within days.

There – I hope that wasn't all too painfully New Age for you. But if it was, you'll probably have to go back and do it all over again.

18

LIBERATION

from the pain of envy and jealousy

I remember once having just finished a huge gig – lots of loud noise, lots of people and lots of applause all dying away in the distance as I walked to the dressing room – and an old friend of mine, someone I considered of far greater stature and certainly of greater wealth and material success, walked in and hugged me (gingerly on account of the blatant post-gig perspiration factor on my part) without a shred of embarrassment or shame, said, 'Wow, I'm really envious of you!'

And because he felt totally OK about it, so did I. There's nothing to be ashamed of in feeling envious. It's merely part of the natural spectrum of human internal experience. On the other hand, there's everything to be ashamed of in acting destructively upon that envy – towards self or others.

It's quite simple really. You notice the envy. You notice how it feels in your body. You breathe. And you accept it. Or you allow it to overcome you, take you over and drive you to act in destructive ways. One way makes life simple, the other hard. The choice is up to you.

What other people do, to the exclusion of you, whether that be to enjoy relative wealth without sharing it with you, or even to enjoy your lover behind your back without asking your permission, is their business, not yours. (The separate issue of broken promises in respect of the latter example, and the chain of cause and effect that it sets in motion, falls into a different area of discussion entirely.)

I remember once (in my mid-30s) being in love to the point of obsession with an extraordinary and beautiful French woman. One night, in the midst of our affair, she arranged to go over to see the guy she'd been having a fearfully destructive relationship with before I'd come along to 'rescue' her (as I mistakenly saw it). When she didn't call me by midnight, I figured they were in bed together but somehow had enough philosophy going for me to fall asleep anyway. At 4am, and I remember it was precisely 4am because for some reason I looked at the clock, I woke up, sitting bolt upright feeling as if I'd just been run through with a sword deep in my guts. I don't mean metaphorically, even though it was – I actually had the physical sensation of being stabbed. I sat there sweating and moaning for a good hour, my distress awaking my psychic faculties, as it does at such times, so it felt like I was actually watching her making love with him, sharing her private self she'd promised to me with him (instead of me, me, me).

At the same time, being a total theatre addict, I couldn't help watching myself going through the drama of it all and beginning to find it quite amusing. In fact, I noticed that when my pride subsided, it was a bit of a turn-on.

After all, to watch this girl in an erotic movie (not that she ever made any) would turn most people on, (men or women), and it was only my pride, itself rooted in delusions of being in competition with all other men and her ex-lover in particular (and that being rooted in a misguided belief about there being only a finite amount of love to go around) that was causing me any problem here.

By the time she did actually phone me from her car at 8am (and I remember it was precisely 8am because for some reason I looked at the clock), I was actually quite composed, emotionally raw, but definitely more enlightened. 'I slept with him, but it's made me really want *you!*' she confessed immediately, and that was good enough for me. 'Good!' I responded (slut that I am), told her of my sword in the gut experience, admitted without embarrassment or shame how I'd been almost struck down by jealousy, and that night had the best sex of the whole affair. (She went away after that and dumped me by phone from the Far East a few weeks later in favour of the ex but shortly after married someone else altogether – as you do.)

Everyone here, including you and your object of jealousy or envy, is each doing their best according to their current state of personal evolution. Though the effects of their process may impinge on you directly or indirectly by triggering your jealousy, it would be delusory to take their actions or superior fortune in the case of envy, personally.

So you feel jealousy and you accept it. 'I feel jealous,' you say, 'and that's alright.' Being ashamed of it, trying to hide or disguise it from yourself or others, merely wastes energy and makes you feel (and look) silly.

Jealousy arises when your liver chi overheats because your kidney chi, normally responsible for keeping the liver cool, is too weak, either through cold climate, stress, a bout of illness, anxiety or the fear of not getting what you need, causes the kidney region to contract.

Conversely, jealousy makes your liver overheat and evaporate the 'water' of your kidneys, thus causing them to weaken and make you feel afraid (of not getting what you need), leaving you more prone to the cold, stress, bouts of illness and anxiety.

To instigate a process of healing for any jealousy attacks you may be suffering and to remove the ground for jealousy attacks to get the better of you in the future, having placed the book somewhere nearby, use the fingertips of your right hand, supported by the weight of your left hand, to press in under your ribs on the right till you feel mildly winded and maintain the pressure there for no more than 50 seconds or so, while breathing out to the sound of *'Shhhhhhhhh!'*

Imagine the sound (being the ancient Taoist liver chi healing sound) is actually escaping through an invisible aperture at the point of fingertip pressure, and carrying with it the poisonous energy of your jealousy as it leaves your body.

Repeat this procedure 3 times or more if feeling particularly jealous. Then remove your fingertips slowly, relax and make something along the lines of the following statement:

'I am willing to trust from now on, that what comes to me is meant for me and what eludes my grasp isn't. I'm also willing to trust that I always get what I need for my personal growth to continue in the healthiest way possible for me and everyone around me.'

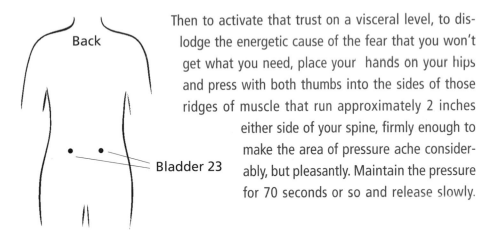

Then to activate that trust on a visceral level, to dislodge the energetic cause of the fear that you won't get what you need, place your hands on your hips and press with both thumbs into the sides of those ridges of muscle that run approximately 2 inches either side of your spine, firmly enough to make the area of pressure ache considerably, but pleasantly. Maintain the pressure for 70 seconds or so and release slowly.

Not only will this help dislodge the fear of not getting what you need that underlies jealousy – it will, over time, if practised with enough adroitness and regularity – among other things it will also help to dislodge and prevent backaches of various sorts, increase your sex drive, boost immune response, relieve constipation and make your thumbs quite strong.

19

LIBERATION

from fear of success

This morning the storm front passed, leaving a sky glistening clear and ice blue above a fresh winter sea stretching silvery into eternity. And as I walk outside tonight a billion, zillion points of light prick clear through the darkness, for there is none of that sickly, reassuring orange glow of city street lights in these parts, the nearest house from here being well over the horizon and the moon almost half empty, only half bright.

A shooting star streaks discreetly across deep space, I make the obligatory wish for all the dreams to (continue to) come true and think of you. I want to tell you one of those stars has your name on it, but it sounds cheesy in my ear, like an ad for the lottery — even though, in a symbolic way, it's true. So I decide not to (but do anyway).

Everyone including you has a lucky star, a guiding light, which if followed in good faith leads to a world where all your wishes come to pass. But you have to believe it. Because like everything in this world of illusions, as you believe, so it will be. And yet you fear it. You fear the very success you wish for.

And why?

Because instinctively you know that maintaining success is much harder work than achieving it in the first place. And losing it once you've had it is more painful than never having it at all. Because you know it will transform you in unpredictable ways and you have grown accustomed to what you've (so far) become. Because it means leaving the soapy, sheltered calm of cul-de-sac reality and exposing yourself to the fierce winds that buffet mountain peaks. Because you know in your bones that success will be no antidote to the terror of the void that always lies beneath all lesser fears. And simply because you, like everyone else, are afraid of change, no matter how potentially liberating its manifestations, nor how enslaving your present condition may be.

You yearn for the liberation of success and yet you fear it at the same time. And that is a very silly way to be. Because one day you're actually going to die. You are not, or are unlikely to be, the one person ever who escapes that fate. Yet I assume by your being here to read this you've managed to overcome your fear of death enough to carry on living till it happens. And that takes great courage.

If you can handle this fear, surely it's only a trifling matter to handle the fear of something so piffling as success and the relatively minor alterations it will make to your circumstances. You'll be able to fly business class instead of economy, drive a Mercedes instead of a Mini, or a Mini instead of a scooter, winter in Fiji instead of the Canaries, and wear mohair and silk instead of microfibres. So what? You'll be seen as (or even become) the proverbial successful asshole. Your friends will be envious of you and more so your enemies. Who cares?

Enough of this fear of success, this fear of expressing fully the unique miracle of who you are, of achieving and manifesting what you've always wanted. As far as you can tell, you only get one go in this insane funfair of a life, so why waste it going round and round on the cup and saucer children's merry-go-round ride, however merry it may be?

Anyone for the big dipper of success, then?

Start by opening your arms wide as if to welcome an old friend and say internally or aloud, as long as not within earshot of anyone with a vested interest in having you sectioned (legally locked up against your will in a mental institution),

'Spirit of Success, I welcome you into all aspects of my life now – come to me (baby), come!'

And don't just say it – feel it. Feel it with all your heart, as the sensation of positivity and optimism floods your chest, fills your belly and lights up your brain. And yes, there is fear. Success will change you, for sure. But fear's only fear and all change is good if you believe it so – say,

'All change is good.'

Good! But now I've roused and enthused you and sold you your own success, you must attend to preparing the optimum energetic internal conditions for your dreams to take form and eventually grow to fruition in the material world. To ring changes in the world around you, begin within.

Knee Acupoints

First, briskly rub with your palms all over the surface of your kneecaps until steaming hot. Then use your thumbs or an improvized poking instrument such as the end of a wooden spoon handle to press firmly into the 'eyes of the knees' – those two indentations below each kneecap, just either side of the mid-line at the very top of each shin – for up to 80 seconds on each of the four eyes, enjoying every moment of the pleasant ache produced, and release.

This unexpected attention to your kneecaps is because your knees are the repository of your fear of change. This is due to your knees' extremely intimate energetic relationship with your kidney chi, which when deficient makes you feel afraid (of anything and everything). As well as being a great way to relieve irksome knee pain, stimulating the chi in your knees in this way helps disperse the fear of change. But don't stop there.

Bending forward from the hips so you can reach round behind you, use your fists to percuss a fast, soft, yet fearsome drum roll on your lower back, one fist pounding either side of your spine for approximately 120 seconds to stimulate the flow of kidney chi in general, thus considerably lessening your fear, and return your torso upright.

Now for your spleen and stomach chi, which corresponds to the earth element and is said to control the flow of material success in your life. Sassy spleen, successful person.

Place your left palm on your upper abdomen just left of centre, take a deep breath and while pushing your right palm slowly and softly away from your chest straight out in front of you in the manner of a policeman stopping traffic in slow motion, chant in as deep and resonant a tone you can muster, the ancient Taoist stomach chi healing sound, *'Shiiiiiiiiiiiiiiii!'*

As you breathe in again, draw your right palm slowly back to your chest to begin another cycle.

Repeat 7 sequences of sound and hand movement, slowly lower both hands and amidst the aftershock vibrating in the ensuing silence, spend a few moments or more daydreaming uninhibitedly about how success will feel, smell, taste, sound and look like (to you).

Then, pressing lightly on the centre of your forehead just below your front hairline in a small indentation you'll find if you feel around for it, which point is said to put you in command of your destiny, say,

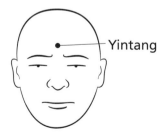

Yintang

'I am a warrior. I can do it.'

Then all you have to do is do it.

LIBERATION

from your internal slave driver

Today, instead of booting up immediately to write, I booted up in the old-fashioned way, went outside, stood amongst the scrub and six wild horses side-lit by the almost blinding low-angle brightness of the sun, and with the boss of the horses nuzzling up to my shoulder and gently biting my upper arm through my jacket, I gazed out at a fishing boat skirting the faintly polluted line of the horizon and began to do tai chi.

Very slowly.

They're fuckers those horses, a bit like Walter the Taoist Dog licking my face when I'm trying to do a (yogic) corpse pose on the floor, or my kids when they were babies, hanging on to my ankles with me trying to step through the (tai chi) form without falling over. But they (the horses) didn't quite manage to knock me over and I came to the end of the form in a relatively graceful fashion, did my best to send out some heal-ing energy to the world, especially to the war zones, though with some resistance letting that awareness into this wild Welsh tranquillity, said 'Ciao!' to the horses in a voice parodying the combined vocal sounds of Barry White and Giorgio Armani on dodgy acid, chuckled to myself and made to return to the barn to de-boot and re-boot in the post-modern sense – start writing in other words.

Not that I felt like it. I just wanted to stay out in the sun, do some Pa Kua, maybe walk up the mountainside, but the tyrant within (who sits atop the adrenals just behind the stomach), was nudging me and not as pleasantly as the horses.

No, this bastard had an agenda. He wanted me finished with this book and out of that barn as quickly as possible so he could push me onto the next project without wasting any more time, and so on, until I was dead and then he could jump into someone else's body and start all over again.

But do you ever wonder who this inner tyrant is? Is he just a sadistic devil who gets off on driving people till they drop? Or is he the archetypal, a priori spirit of progress who drives us all for the greater evolution of the species? Is he your internalized mother, father, priest or primary school teacher? Or is he just a figment of your imagination?

Well whoever he is, I told him to piss off, turned around, walked back to the horses, said 'Ciao!' again, this time like Prince Charles, chuckled once more and began to spin in the manner of a Pa Kua master (or mistress) for a good half hour. And I didn't stop there, but went into a full-blown orgy of hsing i and white crane before trundling up the mountainside, equine buddies in tow, to try and get a signal on my mobile so I could make a call and see if my healing energy had had any effect on the world yet. But coverage was there none, so I came back in, grunted a salutary greeting at the tyrant and started writing. (As you can see.)

You see it's all a matter of balance. You have to balance your internal child with your internal tyrant if you want to get things done and enjoy yourself while you do them.

Sometimes the balance swings one way, sometimes the other, but to get it to steady up somewhere in the middle for appreciable enough lengths of time to attain and maintain peace of mind for the duration, which after all is what you really want above and beyond all else, you may like to experiment with what follows.

To soften and relax the energy of your adrenals, on top of which your inner tyrant perches, enough that he sinks in and disappears into the depths of your kidneys, there to be integrated with your will-power, sitting down or standing up, place hands on hips and press firmly with thumbs into the outer edges of the ridges of muscle that run down either side of your spine. Press firmly enough to produce a strong but pleasant ache, hold for up to 50 seconds and release slowly.

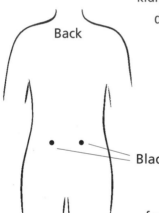

Back

Bladder 23

Now repeat this 2 inches higher up, then stretching your arms high above your head while inhaling deeply, drop slowly forward from the hips (only as far as is comfortable without straining your back), while chanting in the deepest, most resonant tone possible, the ancient Taoist kidney and adrenal chi healing sound, *'Fffuuuuiiiiiiiiiiiii!'*

Repeat this stretch, drop and *'Fffuuuuiiiiiiiiiiiiiiii!'* routine no more than 6 times, then sit back and relax, while autosuggesting,

Back

Bladder 20

''t's perfectly OK for me to go at a comfortable pace. The more comfortable my pace the more I get done.'*

Then spend a moment imagining how that looks, for as you see it, so shall it be.

Next, place a warm palm over your solar plexus (central upper abdominal area) and with the heel of your hand, rub no more than 36 times in slow-motion circles, first anti-clockwise (to dispel stagnant chi, then clockwise to induce fresh chi), moving the flesh firmly against the stomach.

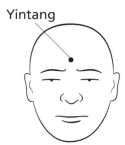

Yintang

Finally, place the tip of your dominant index finger in the slight indentation dead centre of your forehead, just above the line of your eyebrows and press lightly while making tiny circles in a clockwise direction no more than 81 times. This is your 'Happy Point', stimulation of which unifies mind, body, energy and spirit – pulls you together into a definable shape all going in the same direction, in other words. Release the pressure and withdraw your finger gracefully in slow motion so it still feels like you're pressing for a few moments after you've stopped, and while enjoying that sensation (of chi), take a long, full breath and declare,

'From now on, I will only go at a pace I'm comfortable with. This will neither lead to sloth nor entropy but to accomplishing everything I need for healthy growth easily, effortlessly and even miraculously. So be it.'

And so be it.

21

LIBERATION

from holding a grudge

It could be a grudge against a person, a group of people, an entire nation, a corporation, a governing body, the system in abstract or just life in general. It could be specific. It could be random. It could be a chip on the shoulder or a plank in the gut. But whatever it is, it's not doing you any good.

You hold a grudge when an issue or event leaves you angry and unresolved. You then vainly attempt to resolve it by internalizing those you feel wronged you (directly or indirectly) and proceed to punish them by bombarding them (internally) with negative, destructive chi.

However, what you internalize becomes part of you (obviously), so it's not 'them' you're punishing with this destructive chi, but you – your own daft self. That's why people who bear grudges for years and years are such miserable gits, prone to illness and stress and unable ever to truly let go and have a good time.

It's impossible to truly let go and have a good time and still hold onto a grudge. Because to truly let go, you have to truly let go of everything that's hanging you up from otherwise doing so and there's nothing hangs you up more than a grudge – except perhaps adolescent complexes, but we'll come to them later.

Like any other more physical toxin, the energy of grudge sits mostly in your colon, festering away and poisoning your system. To instigate the process of releasing it, close your thumb up to your hand. Looking at the back of your hand you'll see a crack formed between thumb and hand, at the end of which, the flesh of your hand is now protruding. Using the thumb of your other hand, press firmly and purposefully into this protruding flesh at the end of the crack, directing your thrust through the hand towards the centre of your palm. You may have to feel around for the exact point but when you find it, a strong but pleasant, mildly paralysing ache will occur at the site and radiate throughout your hand. The more ache (within reason) you can produce the better, so maintain pressure for as long as you can bear it, but not more than 2 minutes, and then repeat on the other hand.

Lower Intestine 4

This point is famously called your 'Great Eliminator', it being a key player as far as large intestine meridian points go, stimulation of which encourages your colon to eliminate stagnant waste in both physical and energetic form.

While basking in the relief of the aftermath (of pressing the point), focus on all or any grudges you've been holding and, placing your dominant palm across your lower abdomen below the navel, your other hand on top of that, and breathing slowly and fluidly, circle them in a clockwise direction no more than 81 times around your entire abdomen, moving your outer flesh firmly against your innards. As you do, imagine all the stagnant energy of grudges being massaged out through your rectum like a long etheric fart.

Incidentally, this is also an effective way to prevent or ease irritable bowel, constipation, indigestion, flatulence and even baby colic (performed very gently from newborn onwards), as well as being good for boosting sexual energy deficit.

Now arrange yourself in a state of comfortable repose, think of those for whom you've been holding a grudge and, placing them before you in your mind's eye, tell them,

'*Sentence is lifted!*'

See them turn around and walk away and vanish in the distance. Then shake the energy off your hands, like shaking off water, shudder if you feel you want to, raise your arms and shout,

'*Yippee, I'm free!*'

22

LIBERATION

from worrying about social status

I've just been given a tour of Jeb's greenhouses. With their own spring, hydroelectric power, the vast array of juicy fruit and vegetables growing in those greenhouses, and their huge and comprehensive collection of books and music from all the world's great cultures, Jeb and Mike could thrive indefinitely up here, surrounded by enough rugged wilderness to deter the most intrepid of marauders – if the entire global infrastructure should ever break down.

And, in the unlikely but possible event that that should happen, Jeb and Mike would be queen and king for miles around. True, they still wouldn't be able to get a mobile phone signal, but by then it would be of no use anyway. Their rustic set-up would be the epitome of splendour and luxury. They would be the 'it' couple that everyone wanted to know.

Meantime (fortunately for both Jeb and Mike, who only want a quiet life, and for all the rest of us who quite like things the way they are), it is the Hollywood film stars, New York socialites, London celebrities, pop stars, (fashion) models, couturiers, hairdressers, the occasional healer, the occasional ex-world leader, a few ex-gangsters and whatever old-time aristocracy is still somehow managing to hang on in there, who are society's fêted few.

The rest of us merely watch the action on TV, read about it in tabloids and gossip mags, and pretend. It's a silly old game and one that is easy to be distracted by. It's a game where the winners are celebrated (envied, admired, emulated or all three) for what they, their parents or their ex or current partners have or have done, by others who wish they could have or could have done similar, but either don't think they can, for whatever reason, or pretend to themselves and their immediate circle they have or have done similar.

And that's a silly old explanation of a silly old game that you can't get away from – people are programmed to act this way, it's an essential part of how we organize ourselves in groups, sociologically speaking – everyone wants to be somebody.

But imagine wanting to be nobody.

Imagine the relief of walking along the busy street of life being simply nobody. Not having to carry the heavy burden of the myth of who you think you've become (in relation to society), you'd be free to be like a child, to see every detail of the street afresh. You'd still have to work for a living of course (or go homeless), but you'd no longer be constricted by the need to keep up appearances to prove your social worth. If others insulted you by calling you a nobody, you'd simply agree without taking offence. And the paradox is, as I can tell, having once spent, as a personal experiment with reality, nearly a year without home or status, the minute you surrender to the relief of being nobody, you instantaneously become everybody.

As any good Buddhist will tell you, empty your mind of self and you realize that all along you were, are and will be forever more, the entire universe (lifetime after life-time after lifetime). All this clawing in the ground like chickens and clucking hens for a paltry smidgen of social status, is merely a device we use to distract ourselves from the notion of eternity.

Be nobody, in short, and you become everybody (and everything). And being filled with or composed of wealth like that, you naturally feel like king or queen of the world, no matter what. You may not have the trappings or branded accoutrements to show for it. But what are trappings and brand logos to you when the entire universe is your birthright?

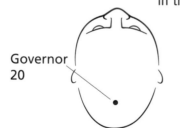

Governor
20

There is a point on the very crown of your head which, if stimulated by press-ing down on it with the tip of your forefinger and then moving that fingertip in tiny clockwise circles so as to move the thin flesh at the crown against the bone beneath no more than 108 times, will produce, within less than 3 or 4 minutes of having been thus stimulated, the momentary effect for you of being both nobody and everybody at the same time.

This is the point which activates the chi of universal consciousness. It is the point through which the spirit within connects with the 'Great Spirit', the Tao, and it empties you of self. Do it now if you like. For as any good, bad or even indifferent Taoist would tell you, when you are empty within, free of the perturbations of status concerns and therefore internally still, your inner space will be so pleasing and hence by extension your external energy field likewise, that even angels, gods and spirits will come to you, let alone mere mortals, because one way or another, vacuums are always filled.

As you circle that fingertip, imagine you are making an opening in the crown of your head, through which you're breathing in and out – all vainglorious thoughts of self escaping with the out-breath and the creativity of the angels, gods and spirits (the Tao) entering and flooding your brain on the in-breath.

Then slowly remove your finger from your head and look about you, imagining the entire world at your feet and say (again) proudly, enough times for it to penetrate so you actually have a moment of feeling it,

'I am king [or queen] of no matter what!'

23

LIBERATION

from worrying about whether you're attractive enough

Everyone wants to look good. There's a whole global media and advertising industry that knows that and how to use it to hook you into buying things. And the hook is self-esteem deficit.

Self-esteem deficit, innate shame about who you are, probably starts somewhere around the time of potty training when you are made to realize more or less delicately by those caring for you that your shit, your piss and your vomit, the visible produce of your body, is something dirty, smelly and to be ashamed of and to hide. This is why, for example, you lock toilet doors to uphold the illusion you don't do such filthy things yourself (only others do), when in fact we all, except possibly the queen, take an average of two shits and six pees a day and vomit once every couple of years at the very least.

Had we not this hang up about our bodily secretions and smells, the toiletries industry would be laying off a lot of people with great alacrity right now. As it is, it's one of the biggest industries there is and it is set to keep growing. And that's not such a bad thing (if you ask me), or what a smelly bunch of animals we'd be. Nonetheless, it's likely that the more wisdom and sensitivity displayed by your carers around the potty training phase (and before), and the less hung up they themselves were about it, the less would be your innate shame and the stronger your basic sense of self-esteem.

When puberty first stirs and adolescence approaches, with its acne, puppy fat, pubic hair sprouting, breasts growing (either not fast and large enough or too fast and too large), penises and facial hair growing or not growing likewise, hormones in turmoil producing uncontrollable mood swings along with the general awkwardness and heightened self-consciousness that accompanies it, just at the time you're taking your first tentative often clumsy and painful steps into the socio-sexual arena, this shame which by now has been locked away behind the toilet doors of your unconscious, resurfaces as an overall emotionally crippling lack of self-esteem and personal vanity. And it continues, masked but prevalent, throughout your adult life until you die or become enlightened about it.

And indeed all the gym owners, beauty, hair care and toiletry product manufacturers, beauticians, hairdressers, manicurists, pedicurists, plastic surgeons, botox merchants, make-up artists, fashion designers, car manufacturers and manufacturers, retailers and service providers of any product you buy because you feel personally insufficient without it, along with the advertising and media industry that depends on you doing so for its revenue, thank you for it. Essentially, with rare exception, in our culture at least, no one fundamentally feels attractive enough.

Moreover, it has little to do with how attractive others actually feel or perceive you to be. I've treated many people for self-esteem deficit over the years including one who was without doubt one of the most physically beautiful women I've ever seen (and I've got a good eye), who was so convinced she was ugly she was on the brink of suicide because of it. And this extreme version of the syndrome is more widespread than you'd imagine. Conversely, I've often come across, as I'm sure you have yourself, many people who are in no way conventionally beautiful, sometimes even downright conventionally ugly, but who are so attractive, charismatic and sexy they can have anyone they want.

It's all down to getting your 'mojo' working, and that requires three things: reduce the personal shame factor, increase the self-acceptance and esteem factor and activate the personal magnetism and general sexiness factor.

Of course, you're not going to sort this out in 5 minutes, it will be an ongoing process till you die, but start by taking Bach Flower remedy of crab apple for the shame (a few drops a day will do), and performing the following exercise to strengthen your spleen chi, which governs your ability to accept yourself.

Take in a long, slow breath, raise your right hand to the side of your forehead like a soldier saluting and with your left hand by your side, turn slowly at the waist approximately 30 degrees to your left, while chanting in the deepest, most resonant tone you can, the ancient Taoist spleen chi healing sound, *'Hhuuuuuuuuu!'* Now turn your waist back to the right to straighten yourself while breathing in again.

Repeat this cycle up to 6 times, then relax your body and mind completely and say,

'It's fine for me to feel ashamed of what I am as long as I find it enjoyable and rewarding, otherwise it's perfectly OK for me to feel proud if I want.'

(Trust me on that one, your unconscious mind will love it).

Next, to boost your heart protector chi, which governs your ability to love in general and yourself in
particular, turn your right palm up and trace a line
from its centre (the stigmata point) to the faint criss-
crossed horizontal line that separates your arm from
your wrist like a bracelet and, where those two lines
intersect in the centre of your wrist, press down
firmly with the thumb of your left hand for no more
than 70 seconds, release and repeat on the other
hand. As you press, think to yourself, *'My inner
beauty shines through my eyes and lights up my
features. I love what I am!'*

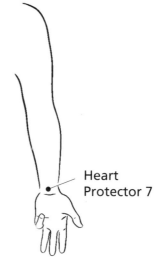

Heart
Protector 7

Paying attention to external factors, such as regular toning exercise, facial
stretches, using good skin products, having your hair done properly, applying
make-up carefully where appropriate, wearing clothes that flatter your shape
in colours that set you off right, and spraying fine scent discretely about your
person, will all help too – as long as you hold them in perspective as ritualis-
tic triggers to remind you to access your inner beauty and not rely on them to
do all the work for you. It's not the surface but what informs it, in other
words.

Finally, to activate your mojo, imagine a breathing aperture in the heel of each foot opening to a channel that runs up the inside of each leg into the perineum between your legs, then continues in a single stream either to the tip of your uterus or the tip of your penis, depending on what kind of day you're having. Now trace your mind back down to your perineum and imagine the channel splitting in two once more, each going along the inguinal canal (the groove that separates thigh from torso) on their respective sides, down the outside of each leg and into the heel of each foot.

Breathe in now and imagine the breath entering through both heels, travelling up the inside of each leg into the perineum and up to the tip of whichever kind of genitals you possess. Breathe out and imagine the breath dropping back down to your perineum, splitting into two streams along the inguinal canals and dropping down the outside of each leg into your heels.

Repeat this cycle no more than 9 times and each time the breath rises towards your genitals say,

'I'm sexy.'

Each time the breath drops back down the outside of your legs say,

'I'm magnetic.'

When you've finished, stand up and say,

'Attractive enough? I'm so damn sexy and magnetic I could eat myself!'

24

LIBERATION

from feeling like you're always in a rush

I've said it before and due to the magnitude of its import will no doubt say it again, but you're aware I presume, I mean viscerally aware, that the approximate bit of planet you're now sitting on, lying down on (or standing on if aboard a crowded train) as you read these words, is currently rotating at a cool and steady 1,000 miles an hour about the planet's axis, which, though admittedly slightly slower than Concorde, is faster than all other forms of commercial transport available to you, unless, of course, you're a billionaire going up in a rocket for a space station vacation.

At the same time (as you read this), you are being transported through deepest, darkest space in an orbital trajectory around the sun and will more than likely continue to be, as if on a cosmic waltzer in perpetual motion, every hour from now on until you die, at the staggering rate of 66,000 miles per hour.

And yet, you still insist on rushing around? 66,000 miles per hour works out at around 19 miles per second. We're talking London to Manchester or, better still, Paris, in under 10 seconds. Isn't that quick enough for you?

This morning I woke with the dawn, did a bit of Taoist yoga to loosen my joints and kick start the flow of blood into my muscles, a round of white crane (shadow boxing) practice to prepare myself for the unlikely event that I should be set upon by a band of brigands on the road and, wrapping my person in many layers, stepped outside into the brain-piercing winter sun to trundle up and over the mountain to the nearest village to pick up a signal on my mobile, check my messages, eat some breakfast and read a newspaper to check if the world of humans was still in business or had blown itself up yet – in which case I would consider delaying my return to London a while longer than initially anticipated.

Afterwards I sat on a bench in the sun, made some calls and waited for the bus to take me to the end of the track that leads back up the mountain to the barn and another round of creative isolation. The bus ride cost 52p, incidentally (the best part of a euro or dollar) – 52p, not 50p or even 55p. People here still have enough sense of perspective to value pennies. And you know why? Because they're not in a rush.

I mention this because it illustrates how, as you rush more, you haven't got time to concern yourself with pennies, you have to round things off to the nearest five or ten, you tend to value detail less and less. Details such as those two little pennies cease to have significance to you and could therefore be said to no longer exist. And if, as the cliché goes, the Devil is in the detail, you're progressively diminishing your chances of enlightenment with every detail lost to your awareness.

That 52p revelation and the trek I made to get it means I'll now probably finish writing this book (to you) approximately five hours later than scheduled. And that means I'll either have to stay up all night or break into the next day when I'm actually due back in the thick of the mêlée with all my wits about me.

But that doesn't mean I have to rush now. Rushing would only make my head spin and make me incapable of thinking clearly enough to write, which would paradoxically slow me down and force me to extend further this phase of creative confinement, which in turn would throw my entire finely-tuned and balanced schedule into disarray for weeks to come. In fact, the only expedient thing to do is to slow down even more. To relax my muscles, relax my brain and slow down my breathing so that my head clears and the words flow fast. The alternative would only lead me to panic, which would bring my creative flow to a swift, sudden and irksome end.

Rushing is habit-forming (as any pill-head will tell you). It may feel good the first time. Maybe even the first few times. But after a while you become habituated to it, don't even notice you're doing it and any enjoyment you initially felt is gone. Maybe you started rushing in the first place with the good intention to get all your business done as quickly as possible so you could sit back and relax for longer. But as soon as the addiction kicks in (often as early as the first or second time you do it), you can't stop rushing around even when you've got time to sit and do absolutely nothing and have absolutely nothing to do. You'll find things to do.

Maybe you started rushing to keep up with the demands of others – your parents, your partner, your children, your friends, your boss – which was very considerate (and silly) of you to be sure, but, as you've probably noticed, the more you rush about for them, the less quality attention you are able to give them, which may ultimately reduce you to a such nervous, agitated and quivering wreck that your parents disown you, your partner leaves you and takes the children, your friends desert you and you get fired. (So slow down, will you?)

Say immediately before it's too late, '*This is my life, my time, and I'll do with what I choose*.' And let me be so bold as to suggest you choose to stop rushing as of ... now. The tendency to rush occurs when your kidney region contracts (producing fear, in this case, of not keeping up), causing your adrenal fire to burn too hot, (putting that hot banana up your arse).

Conversely, when you habitually rush, it causes your kidneys to contract and hence their chi to be squeezed upwards into the adrenals above ('renus' is Latin for kidney and 'ad' means next to – they are adjacent to your kidneys), causing them to overheat, which in turn makes you want to rush about (either in your head, around the house or out on the street) even more.

To reverse this tendency and thus liberate yourself for evermore from feeling you're always rushing, start by placing your hands on your hips and pressing your thumbs into the sides of the ridges of muscle that run either side of your spine, which (on having felt around sufficiently to find the right point) will produce a strong but pleasant (if you relax and don't resist) ache. The stronger the contraction, the stronger the ache. The longer and stronger you can take the ache, the quicker you'll release the contraction. Maintain this pressure without holding your breath for approximately 80 seconds and release slowly, focusing your awareness on the contraction letting go.

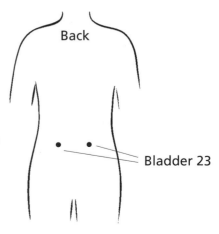

Back

Bladder 23

Next, slow your breathing tempo down to half speed, and with a palm on your belly to remind you, concentrate on making the breath fluid (no holding it before the out-breath, in other words), regulated (steady tempo with inhalation and exhalation of equal duration), deep (so the movement of your diaphragm makes your belly expand as you inhale and contract as you exhale), smooth (like a fine, round string of pearls) and silent. As the breath, so the mind and so the chi. (And there's nothing worse than being around someone with a held-back, uneven, shallow, rough and noisy mind – or chi, for that matter. It gets right on your nerves.)

Complete up to 9 full breath cycles like this then remove your palm and, raising it to shoulder height like a president being sworn in, make this vow (if you want),

'I vow from now to only ever take things at a pace I enjoy and am comfortable with. The more I enjoy my pace and feel comfortable with it, the faster I can go and the more effective I will be in the long run. Any good downhill skier will tell me that!'

Finally, thinking of all the things you have to get done next and the time you've allotted for doing them, place your palms together in front of your chest, imagining you hold that space of time between your hands with the beginning point attached to the centre of one palm and the end point attached to the other, slowly draw your hands apart, as if stretching time, until your hands are a full arm span apart and say,

> *'I now choose to stretch this time in order to fit everything*
> *in easily, effortlessly, enjoyably and even miraculously. I am*
> *now amazed by how much I can accomplish.'*

And you will be.

25

LIBERATION

from the system

That's easy. There is no system. You just think there is.

The system, so called, is in fact just six billion people globally who have managed, following on a long line of ancestors who have progressively managed likewise as the aeons roll by, to organize themselves more or less efficiently by forming groups within groups within groups within groups and so on, some of which are labelled, say, 'government departments', some 'multinationals', some 'the police', some 'the army', some 'the tax office', some 'the health service', some 'public transport', some 'the high street retailers', and some 'the corner shop down the road'. But no matter how slickly or not they present themselves with logos and brand names, uniforms and jargon, these groups within groups are comprized of nothing more than people. People who love and fear, sleep and wake up, go to work and come home, get born and die, just like you and me.

Organizing ourselves as a species, is a function of nature to promote our survival. We are interdependent beings. And no one is exempt, however hard you try to be (a hermit). And that includes you, (buddy). You are the system too. To want to be free of the system per se is to want to be free of yourself. And for now that's entirely impossible.

Instead, see through the illusion you've constructed, even if it's one constructed by many others too and see the truth, which is that there is no system. All there is, is lots of people. And you know how to handle them.

Be thoughtful, be kind, be polite, show you care.
Be awake, be alert, and you'll get by anywhere.

(Say, '*I'm thoughtful, I'm kind, I'm polite, and I care. I'm awake, I'm alert, I get by everywhere.*')

Feelings of 'rage against the machine', of alienation from what you perceive to be the system, but which is in fact just other people organizing themselves in various ways, and wanting to liberate yourself from them (all), probably starts soon after birth and grows thereafter as you rage against your mother for not being perfect or some such other heinous crime, (and then wishing to be free of her.)

The 'system' is therefore your mother. The globally organized activities of humans on the planet, is after all, what's keeping you alive one way or another. The system is the breast you feed upon, so don't be angry with it. Don't try to abandon it. Be kind to it, and say, '*I love you mummy*'. And it will be kind to you.

Meantime, place your right palm over your front lower left ribs and rubbing round and round in approximately 81 small, quick clockwise circles, moving flesh firmly against bone. This will stimulate your spleen chi, which, being associated with the earth element, is responsible for seeing you get everything you need through your dealings with other people on the planet.

When your circles stop, rest your palm there and allow the heat generated to penetrate into your spleen, which sits beneath those ribs, and say,

'Thank you'.

26

LIBERATION

from making sense

'Ichne laterondi natalion kedumso, ess nachtali inso dus laya in fuschd.'

There now, that wasn't so unsettling to read, was it? I would like to tell you that it was some strange old Celtic, middle European or ancient Aryan spell to bring you as much money, sex, and nice shoes as you can handle for evermore without any come-back. Had I told that, you'd have been suspicious but none the wiser, until some eagle-eyed boffin wrote in to the tabloids complaining and bringing about my sudden downfall, exposed as a gobbledegook-peddling fraud. But had I and had you believed me, your mind would already be trying to make sense of it, as it tries to with most of the other worthless gobbledegook that is peddled its way these days under the banner of post-modern 'culture'.

Of course, there is sense. There is an innate sense in the way the Tao manifests reality for you, if you're only willing to stop trying to make sense of it all, relax, trust, observe, discern, but not seek to draw conclusions. There are no conclusions. We live in an eternal continuum. When you die, the energy that was you, merely goes and fills the next available vacuum. Nothing ends, it just undergoes transformation. Any good physicist will tell you that. It all goes round and round, just like the planets go round the stars, forever and ever. So what's the point of trying to label it all and stick it in neat little boxes? It (the Tao) just won't fit.

This need to organize reality into boxes, arises when your spleen chi, which is responsible for the good working order of your intellect, heats up and goes into hyperdrive. This in turn causes you to over-intellectualize about things and vainly attempt to order them. However, if you step back, get your intellect out of the equation and give them space to do so, things order themselves each according to its individual Tao (way) into a state of perfect harmony.

To assist you in this, plunge the fingertips of your left hand, supported by the weight of your right, in under the ribs on your left (front) side until feeling the ache of contraction as fingertips touch overcompressed spleen. (Spleen chi overheats when this region is overly compressed or contracted. Contraction squeezes this hot chi up into your brain, which makes you think 'too much'). Maintain meaningful pressure for no more than 80 seconds or so and release slowly. As you do, imagine all excess intellectual energy (spleen chi) drop down from your brain, through your throat and the left side of your chest behind your heart and into the spleen region (which you've just been pressing and which has now been decompressed affording you an expanded space in which to receive and hold that energy.)

Then, for the next 2 or 3 days, or an appreciable length of time, attempt to draw no conclusions, label, judge or pass sentence on life: just let it happen as it will. Say,

'The less sense I try to make of life, the more sense it will make.'

Then say,

'Ichne laterondi natalion kedumso, ess nachtali inso dus laya in fuschd'.

You never know, it might work.

27

LIBERATION

from being stuck in a duff relationship

That's easy.

You just collect your bits and pieces, walk to the door, put your hand on the door handle, turn or pull it as appropriate, open the door wide enough to get you and your belongings through it, turn and say, 'See you around,' turn again and walk. And keep walking till you see your car, a cab, or some form of public transport to take you and your belongings, if you don't feel like walking all the way, to your home or some other safe harbour, thence to despoil and regroup while making sure not to succumb to temptations to return whether by your instigation or theirs until sufficient time has passed for you (both) to conduct all further dialogue with each other on a non-intimate basis, which includes being able to handle discussing any developments (or lack of them) in your personal lives from the moment of your leaving up until that meeting, should indeed you (both) wish to have one.

However, for this you will need to access clarity (to know that you want out one hundred per cent), strength (to carry your belongings), resolve (to see your decision through in the face of the pain of breaking the addiction to being with them, for however duff it has been, you always get addicted to some degree), courage (to face and feel the pain of change), faith (it will all work out – for both of you), trust (in reality to bring you everything you need now for your healthy growth, including being happy on your own or meeting someone else), will-power (to stay away from each other afterwards), communication skills (to negotiate, as appropriate, the fair distribution between you of income, goods, chattels and home or homes, as well as custody and access rights in relation to children and pets – including goldfish and terrapins), compassion (both for you and they for having to go through the pain of change), grace (to appreciate the time you spent together, otherwise you've just devalued a precious sequence of time in your life, and seeing as in one way, ultimately, time is all you have, that would be silly), and a sense of humour (so when you're talking it all over with your friends for the eighty-sixth time you can sprinkle a few good gags in here and there lest you bore them all half to death and end up with no one to hang out with).

To trigger that, start by taking many drops of Bach Flower remedy of walnut hourly to help you through such times of transition, repeating as you swallow, *'All change is good'* over and over till it becomes like the pattern on the cereal bowl of your mind.

Stabilize your emotions by doing as many upper body strengthening exercises, (push-ups, yogic crab, yogic hand balances, free weights, rowing, for example), as you can think of, as much of the time as you can. Between each bout of whichever form or combination of forms of exercise you do, suggest to yourself, *'I am now stabilizing my emotions – I handle this entire transition with aplomb',* it being important that you give yourself a lot of self-empowering chat through such times, to keep your otherwise over-stretched and emotionally distracted mind working in at least a semblance of a straight line, so to speak.

Look, it's horrible. There's no point saying otherwise. Separation (with anyone, anything, anywhere, or even 'anywhen', you love in the broader sense) is what causes all the pain round here, other than the cruelty of people to each other, stubbing your toe (especially if you're barefoot) and that kind of thing. That's why the Buddha made such a big deal about developing non-attachment, teaching it was (and is) the only way to avoid suffering. Which is all well and good for that little fat dumpling of spiritually sound geezer – he wasn't coming out of a duff relationship. For you it's too late for that. You've already become attached.

But as you cut those (imaginary) 'ties that bind you' and the pain sears through your heart knocking your heart pro-tector chi sideways, press hard with right thumb into centre of left palm and vice versa to straighten that chi out and take solace from the fact that approximately 90 days from now, give or take a month or two, you (and hopefully they) will be feeling right as rain.

Heart Protector 8

In the meantime, see it like having very bad flu. The first three days are the worst and then it gradually subsides, perhaps with a few bouts of post-viral syndrome when the wobbles come, as they inevitably will.

And when they do, just repeat round and round within, as if the pattern on the entire dinner service of your mind,

'I have the clarity, strength, resolve, courage, faith, trust, will-power, communication skills, compassion, grace and humour to handle this with equipoise and magnanimity for all concerned. I have the clarity, strength, resolve, courage, faith, trust, will-power, communication skills, compassion, grace and humour to handle this with equipoise and magnanimity for all concerned'.

28

LIBERATION

from wanting

You have three possible approaches to this. You can enter a monastery, nunnery or some similar place of permanent retreat and spend the rest of your life meditating on watching the rise and fall of desire, simply watching, gradually achieving larger spaces of time without longing for this or that (money, status, sex mostly), until maybe eventually those spaces join up and form one long uninterrupted experience of not wanting anything – nirvana in other words.

You can spend from now till the end of your life getting the things (possessions, people and experiences), so you don't want them anymore. (You don't want something if you have it because you have it. You only want the things you haven't got – that's what the word 'want' is in the English language for – to convey longing for something presently out of your grasp.)

Or you can combine the two and do what you can to get what you want, while watching from within the internal dialogue that goes on incessantly about what, who, where and how you want what you want and what it feels like once you've got it, while reminding yourself that it's all theatre, and behind all the longing, for no matter what or whom, is the longing to be home – to be at peace with yourself, in other words – and that when you die, what you've wanted and what you've got or had will all vanish as far as you're concerned, all except for that peace.

Longing, yearning, wanting for something or someone is only painful when your spleen chi, which governs being satisfied with where you are, whom you're with and what you're doing in the moment, is weak. Conversely, when longing, yearning and wanting become painful, it weakens your spleen chi, causing feelings of dissatisfaction with where you are, whom you're with and what you're doing, which make you long, yearn and want for something else.

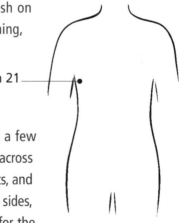

Spleen 21

So, as well as taking a small dab of horseradish on the end of your tongue at 11.00am each morning, (the time your spleen chi is most receptive), the mere taste of which will stimulate spleen chi, and introducing millet into your diet, which is known to help strengthen spleen chi, spend a few moments during the day with your arms folded across your chest, hands tucked tight under your armpits, and where your little fingers touch your ribs on both sides, press in firmly for no more than 40 seconds, or for the length of time it takes to remind yourself lyrically like so:

'Where I am is where I am … meant to be.
When I relax, what I want, is what comes to me.'

(And therein lies the secret, you see.)

29

LIBERATION

from having to be right all the time

Right and wrong are opinions. Right and wrong are relative to the situation and the time. If you kill someone in 'peace time', the powers that be, the law of the land will believe it wrong and punish you for it if they catch you (and quite rightly so, if you ask me, other than for reasons of genuine self-defence where killing is truly the only option available to prevent yourself or someone you've elected to protect from being killed, and may neither you nor I nor anyone we love ever find ourselves in such an position).

However, if you kill someone in 'war time' (someone of the so-called 'other side'), as long as you're both in uniform and operating more or less under orders, the powers that be, the law of the land, will believe it right and you may even win a medal. If even something so extreme and nasty as murder can, in the appropriate set of circumstances, be believed wrong one minute and right the next, then right and wrong are clearly merely relative terms.

The same goes for every other belief you or anyone else may hold. It is, in other words, only a belief, which may be right in one set of circumstances, wrong in another. If you take the circumstances out of the equation, and abstract the issue, a belief you have is not right or wrong, but right *and* wrong. Your ancestors, your parents, your teachers, your priests, your heroes, your role models, your doctors, your barefoot doctors even, your friends, your enemies – all their beliefs and opinions over all these years have all been right and wrong simultaneously, and so have yours.

Liberation, the freedom to enjoy the moment for whatever it offers, can only occur when you stop drawing conclusions about right or wrong and when you stop preferring this over that. When you're finally willing to see all occurrences as mere appearances in a cosmic hall of mirrors, apparently good or apparently bad depending on the camera angle, lighting and context, you'll know that the only true succour is to be found within. So you no longer need defend your beliefs, your opinions nor contend nor fight with others who defend beliefs and opinions different to yours, (unless of course, for whatever unforeseen reason your life or the lives of others you've elected to protect, somehow physically depend on it), because you no longer need be right. You can be wrong. It doesn't matter. You can agree to disagree.

But to be so enlightened in your dealings with others requires you to prevent the chi in your kidneys rising up to your chest like a hot wind, making you top heavy with self-importance and literally act like a (hot) windbag, a condition known as disharmony of fire and water (heart and kidneys in other words), which you can begin to sort out right now by following the following.

Tap out with your fingertips a spritely roll on and all around your inner ankle bones, one foot at a time, for around 60 seconds per foot, to wake up your kidney chi. Bring your fingers and thumbs together at the tips on both hands to form a pair of beak-like shapes. Using the tip of each beak, tap another spritely roll, this time on the centre of your chest, to disperse the hot wind (of bombast). Now place hands on hips and press with your thumbs into the sides of those ridges that run down either side of your spine, 2 or 3 inches either side of it, until producing a strong but pleasant ache. Hold for no more than 70 seconds and release slowly, to make the kidney region relax and create a bit of room in which to catch the above hot wind as it disperses after the spritely drum roll.

Tai chi boxers talk about investing in loss, the art of losing one's self-importance, to become empty of self, so that if struck by an opponent, you feel no pain or humiliation because there's no one there to feel it. By being empty, your mind is receptive to wherever your opponent is going next so you can follow but arrive there first. (This is known as leading from behind).

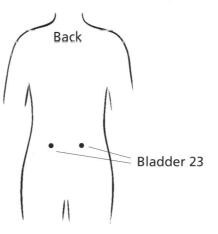

Shake your hands as if shaking all sense of self out through your fingertips until you feel relatively empty, then say,

'I'm not here to be right. I'm not here to be wrong. I'm simply here to be.'

Am I right?

30

LIBERATION

from addiction

Forget it. I'm too addicted myself to help you with that. Addicted to this planet, addicted to people, to breathing, love, feeling safe, feeling warm, companionship, sex, communication, food, tea, water, fruit juice, music, work, success, travel, excitement, adrenalin, thinking, tai chi, feeling good, looking good (in my opinion), smelling good, comfort, civilization, clothes, money, urban pollution (I swear I get lead and carbon withdrawal symptoms out here), time, health, meditation, the very odd drop of Scotch (or Irish), the not so odd drop of THC, acupuncture, being alive in general and even this old, cold, stone barn on its sunlit, (heavily alliterated), wild, windy, wintertime, wondrous, Welsh mountainside. But mostly I, (like you, as well as damn near everyone else round here as far as I can see), am addicted to more. More of everything I like, that is.

I can help you liberate yourself from the addiction to worrying about addiction, but it's impossible to liberate yourself from addiction itself. Addiction is a crucial part of the human drive to thrive. The wanting (more – more excitement, more contentment, more comfort, more ease, more time, more peace, more love and of, course, always more money) is what urges us as a species to progress and develop better tools, better methods, better ideologies, better communications, better organization, better laws, better infrastructure and better means of defending ourselves from people wanting to hijack, appropriate or simply destroy all that better stuff.

True, the process of common betterment may at times appear inexorable and ponderously slow. For example, the majority of our world's population still exists below the poverty line while the minority (us) live like lords and ladies (moaning because life's so damn tough, the trains don't run on time, security delays at the airport are insufferable, there's nothing much good on TV and house prices have become absolutely ridiculous). Too many crazed, cruel, twisted, violent people are still compelled to act out their inner distortions; levels of corruption and folly of global proportions still infiltrate society all the way down from the highest levels of government; we still go at a tortoise-like pace in developing and adopting sustainable energy sources; and the apparently insatiable appetite of the military-industrial complex still fuels the continual 'need' for war to be 'happening' somewhere on the planet (as far away from military-industrial complex hubs as can be reasonably managed, of course, in order to safeguard the finance it generates, which along with currency trading, stocks and shares, porn, prostitution, drugs and a few other odds and bobs like technology, food and oil trading, keeps the global economy afloat).

Still, looking back over known history, we've come a long way since the days (and nights) when we lived in caves. Ergo, in the balance, your addiction to more life and more of everything it offers is a healthy one. In any case, it's not a matter for debate – addiction was organically wired into your circuitry at the time of conception, as one cell divided to make two because one was simply not enough, and more and more, until there were so many cells they no longer sat comfortably together in your mother's uterus and you were born. However, the problems begin when your addictions become unbalanced, when you focus all your wanting more, on one bit of fruit in the basket to the exclusion of all others, say in the case of wanting more and more of a drug until you have time to want or do nothing else (including eating), and you die.

What we're talking about here is managing your addiction (to, say, drugs, tobacco, alcohol, porn, destructive relationships, sex, masturbation, painkillers, money, work, shopping, shoplifting, crisps, chocolate, sugar, starving yourself, inflicting or submitting to physical pain for kicks and so on and so on) so that it's evenly balanced and spread in its focus to include addiction to such things as daily exercise, yoga, tai chi, meditation, acupuncture, massage, reflexology, craniosacral therapy, hypnotherapy, psychotherapy, thinking optimistically, getting lost in creative pursuits, being kind to people, others being kind to you or you being kind to yourself, to name but a few examples, at which point and thereafter, if you continue to so manage it, your addiction will no longer present a problem, then recede from your awareness and thus be then said to no longer exist. And through rebalance comes liberation.

As any ancient Taoist tell will you, to achieve balance in your addiction, so that your focus of wanting (more) is evenly spread over all the fruits (as well as spices) in the basket that you need for your ongoing healthy growth, it is best to withdraw your attention completely from pondering the negative and destructive aspects of yourself and refocus instead on the positive and regenerative. For what you focus on grows.

In other words, focus your attention on increasing and developing your positive addictions and the negative ones will take care of themselves (if you let them). No matter the addiction or addiction-combination, what you are doing every time you take a hit, fix, snort, gulp, gobble or what-have-you is (unconsciously) taking the nipple (of your mother – the 'Great Mother', life, the Tao or however you wish to see it) and sucking it.

And the reason you like to recreate (unconsciously) the sensation of suckling like that is because it was the first tangible, visceral relief that came after the discomfort and tears of newborn hunger and sometimes (cot-bound) isolation. It reminded you of the good old golden age (in the womb before you were too big to swim around in there) and was a reliable way of spending some quality time with yourself (in the arms of the mother or whoever) and you got addicted. So you (unconsciously) perpetuate your addiction in order to recreate a moment of being in touch with yourself, with the Tao (or she who provides for your well-being).

Therefore, the more you now explore and develop different, healthier ways to get in touch with yourself, your need for unconsciously acting out the breast-sucking scenario in destructive ways, progressively weakens. Conversely, as you allow yourself to be conscious of the fact that every time you take a hit of the breast in the destructive way, you are actually calling to the Tao, the 'Great Mother' or your own higher self, as you prefer, for a moment of succour for your spirit. Even these destructive tendencies (of yours) become moments of meditation that can reinforce you.

In the same way Reiki healers channel energy into their food before eating it, or in the way people from many religions bless their food before eating, if you declare, before taking say, a drag of a fag or a nostril full of cocaine, '*I am doing this to make contact with my higher self*', it at least attenuates the psychological and hence energetic damage otherwise done by feeling guilty and ashamed about it. You may also find, that 'spiritualizing' the act, however otherwise destructive, will invite your 'higher self', spirit or Big You (your god in other words) into the equation, and you are quite likely to become addicted to that instead. Or you could just say that the more time you spend doing things that are good for you (including freeing yourself of worrying about addiction), the less time you'll have to spend doing things that aren't, as there are only 24 hours in a day, or so they say.

To which end, start now by rising slowly to your feet, which should be placed as if standing on two parallel train tracks, bend your knees, allow your pelvis to sink, elongate the back of your neck, draw your chin closer to your chest, relax your shoulders, breathe evenly, fluidly and deeply and with tongue touching the roof of your mouth, allow your arms to swing up and down in slow-motion from the shoulders, palms up as your arms raise up, palms down as they drop down again, no more than 180 times, inhaling as your arms raise up, exhaling as they descend.

On every in-breath, suggest to yourself,

> *'I am gorging on healing chi'*

and feel that as the chi fills your chest. On every out-breath, suggest,

> *'I choose my own addiction'.*

Repeat that every day for 90 days and within no time you'll become totally addicted, you'll find yourself wanting to do nothing in your spare time but stand there swinging your arms, and one day you may actually find yourself looking at your life and declaring with gusto,

> *'It don't mean a thing*
> *If it ain't got that swing'.*

31

LIBERATION

from feeling sexually inadequate

To sell copies, achieve ratings, move product and ensure box office receipts, the people who make editorial decisions on the content of newspapers, magazines, books, TV shows, radio programmes, adverts and movies, which between them comprise the way cultural information is fed to your brain, blatantly and subliminally feed you with the optimum amount of sexual content appropriate to their particular mode of delivery at the time, ranging from negligible amounts for the less popular forms of brain feed, such as the broadsheets, to considerable amounts for the more popular forms, such as TV.

This is because everyone on the planet with few exceptions has or has had at some time, a deep-rooted fascination with sex – sex on their own, sex with others, and others' sex. This may well (unconsciously) be because sex, like drugs or alcohol, is an instant way to reach into a state of altered awareness wherein you are briefly relieved of pain and are in touch with the invisible but powerful realm of sensations, which is where you most easily feel the Tao, which, whether you realise it or not, is what everyone instinctively wants to feel.

It may also be because we suppress much energy on a daily basis attempting, mostly successfully, to divert the all-powerful sexual urge, sublimating it as best we can, without which, in a hypothetical world with no social mores and charades, would otherwise have us engaging in coitus with anyone and everyone who took our fancy all day long and we'd get nothing else done. But what happens to all that suppressed energy? It has to find something to lock onto. Something safe that won't get you in trouble. So you lock onto reading about sex, listening to people talk about it, watching people doing it or alluding to it (in adverts, on TV and in movies). Sex is the root force of nature. It's what makes the world go round. It will not be ignored and will draw your attention one way or another, whether you want it to or not. OK, so big deal, we have a publishing, media and advertising industry that relies on sex to sell product and we're all suckered by it (including, incidentally, the people who work in publishing, media and advertising — we're all punters). We all know that.

But what's happened is with all that focus on sex, a lot of nonsense has inevitably been purveyed, especially over the last decade or so, simply because a lot of nonsense is purveyed whatever we're talking about. Human society is like that. And because we always collectively sink to the lowest cultural common denominator, it's usually the nonsense, the sensationalist as opposed to the considered, that sticks in the group psyche. Of course, this could be remedied by enlightened teachers educating their pupils sensitively, comprehensively and realistically about sex and all its aspects from an early age in order to prevent ignorance taking hold from the start.

But until such a time occurs and common sense prevails, we're walking around as confused as hell, our heads filled with unrealistic nonsense full of the highest expectations about how our sexual relationships are meant to be, and on the whole falling short of that. This induces deep-seated feelings of inadequacy in all parties concerned, which causes unnecessary psycho-emotional discomfort. We then walk this discomfort into our sexual liaisons and, like any self-fulfilling prophecy, often find ourselves (and our partners) having third-rate sex.

Obviously, there are a few people around who, for certain parts of their lives, with certain partners to spark them off properly, are veritable sexual deities. There are couples whose sex lives get better and better and who swear they never so much think of someone different. There are people who can do it ten times a day, every day forever and ever and never go flat. There are men (and women) who know women's (and men's) bodies inside out, know their G-spots and all the right triggers to promote clitoral or penile delight and are happy to perform for hour upon hour without getting bored or boring, who have no inhibitions and will do anything and everything imaginable so you can't stop thinking about it or recounting it to your friends for days afterwards.

Yet, though these people, these sexual gods and goddesses are extremely rare, the myth that these are the norm has been so successfully promulgated by the media, that you're now running around town filled with unrealistic expectations of yourself and others and of the whole sexual experience in general, interpreting subjectively and measuring yourself (sometimes literally) against a so-called norm, which inevitably leaves you feeling inadequate.

But you're not. Unless you believe you are. (For as you believe, so shall it be).

Sex, like dancing is a form of self-expression shared (hopefully) with someone else doing likewise. Sometimes you want to express yourself fully, sometimes only a bit. Sometimes you want to express the dark side, sometimes the light. Sometimes you feel loving, sometimes you feel downright filthy. Sometimes you want to express yourself with great frequency, sometimes you just want to keep yourself to yourself. There are no rules.

There can be no rules. Multiply by two (or more depending on the kind of scene you're into) all the variables involved, from fluctuations in hormonal cycles, time of year, climate, health, state of mind, external stress, energy levels, bad hair days, complexes, inhibitions, moods, expectations, changing smells and secretions, as well as environment (emotional and locational), fears of disease or entrapment, the pitfalls of miscommunication, hang-ups from past relationships or sexual trauma, and strange desires that seem to arise from nowhere, and it is a marvel we ever manage to enjoy sex with other people at all, let alone try and universalize the entire, vast, limitless conundrum of an issue in one small chapter.

Your sexual activity on this planet – your prowess, your power, your hunger, your expressiveness, your responsiveness, your performance, your frequency, your sensitivity, your pleasure, your curiosity, your inventiveness and your excitement – is all governed by the strength and quality of chi produced in your kidneys. When your kidney chi is strong and flowing, the sexual urge will find satisfactory expression through you commensurate with the situation you find yourself in. When your sexual energy is weak, it won't. How this manifests in practice depends on the kind of variables mentioned above. But it's safe to say that no matter the glitch, if you do the following to strengthen kidney chi and keep doing it for a few days, your sexual confidence will subtly increase as will your libido. How you then choose to express it is beyond the scope of this book.

With hands on hips, press with thumbs firmly into the outer sides of those ridges of muscles running down either side of your spine, about 2 inches out to the sides, which, if you've been reading the book sequentially, will by now be more than familiar to you. Press till you feel a strong but pleasant ache, which may radiate down towards your sacrum, and maintain pressure for between 70 and 80 seconds before releasing slowly and relaxing your thumbs. This makes your kidneys relax which is the first step in increasing strength and refining quality of the chi they produce.

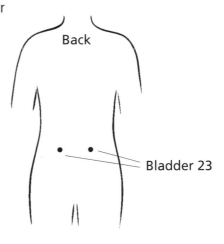

Now, using the backs of your hands, rub briskly and vigorously up and down over the same points, with approximately 4 inches between the upper and lower limits of movement, to generate great heat, then stay your hands and let it penetrate and radiate from your kidneys to your feet.

Next, rubbing your palms together until they grow hot, place them on your pubic bone, fingers reaching down between your thighs, one hand either side of the midline of the pubis, and again, allow the heat to penetrate.

Now, move your palms out over the tops of your thighs, down the outside of your thighs to the outsides of your knees, under the kneecaps and up the inside of your thighs all the way to the perineum between your legs before starting the next cycle, 9 cycles of which, along with all the preceding advice, should suffice to 'awaken the dragon', the sexual fire in your loins and support all your sexual activity for the next 24 hours as if you'd taken Viagra.

The entire procedure repeated daily for 90 days will stabilize your libido and help you harmonize sexually more easily with yourself and partners, as well cause you to give off sexual energetic vibrations that'll attract potential partners to you.

To reinforce this, because as you see it is the way it will turn out to be, memorize and keep repeating till it becomes habitual,

'As I see it is how it shall be. I'm now willing to see myself as a sexually healthy, functional and desirable being, therefore I am one. Others, especially sexual partners see it too. In fact, I'm so sexually healthy, functional and desirable as a being, I'm almost too sexy (for my car, etc) altogether'.

32

LIBERATION

from suicidal tendencies

[This item applies to cases other than when engaging in voluntary euthanasia for valid medical reasons and where legally acceptable.]

One way to liberate yourself from this once and for all is to follow the tendency through to its logical conclusion and commit suicide, preferably without blowing yourself up in a crowded place or causing any vehicles you may have hijacked to crash, especially those carrying other passengers who may not wish to end their lives with you at that moment.

Even keeping it a private affair, there will be those you leave behind who will feel you have violated and killed a part of them also, which may scar them for the rest of their lives – people who love you and who, somewhere in your twisted soul, you love too. But, even if you don't think anyone loves you, by doing yourself in you sever all chances of ever again meeting anyone who will, for opportunities to love and be loved never cease presenting themselves if your eyes are willing to see it.

At the very moment you feel darker inside than the darkest night (of the soul), your anger with the world and subsequent need to punish it is more seething than a nest full of vipers and your prospects are as dim as the night vision of the blindest mole, the exact moment you bottom out is the exact moment grace enters your energy field, as any good mystic will tell you. Hence, were you to end it all now, you can be sure that had you not, the very next moment from now would be the one in which the light would begin to ascend once more. Except you wouldn't be here to see it, feel it, smell it, hear it, taste it and all the other things you do to appreciate light while you still have the rare privilege of having a human body in which to experience such things. And you wouldn't be able to change your mind and come back. You would no longer even have a mind to change. You'd be gone.

But, of course, it's your choice, always. Though when you consider the enormous courage involved in planning and bringing about your death by your own hand, before taking any irreversible steps, it could be prudent of you to spend some time evaluating calmly how your life would be if you were to use that courage constructively instead.

For example, if you were to compose on paper a description of how you'd like your life to go from here were you not about to end it, including feeling light and glad to be alive (because surely you'd like to feel light and be glad to be alive, wouldn't you?), along with all the various factors that would make such a thing possible, and then see yourself accessing that immense courage you must have even to consider taking your own life but employing it instead to making your own life (as you'd really like it if you could have anything you wanted right now – and I mean everything), you would find, no doubt, that even in the short time it would otherwise take for your body to decompose and start smelling awful beyond belief, your life would already be turning around for the better.

There's no mystery about it. According to the time-honoured law of yin and yang, darkness is always followed by light and vice versa. Furthermore, the times in life you face the darkness and don't run away are the times that reward you with the most blessings straight afterwards. But maybe you're just too impatient and maybe I'm just being too sentimental about it. After all, yours is only one life in a world of six billion, so what's the big deal.

It's just that I, like most others, believe that this life is the most miraculous event any of us will probably ever witness, and that seeing as relative to eternity the whole thing is done and dusted in the twinkling of a cosmic eye, over with before you know it, in other words, it would seem impetuous at the least to shorten it even more, however crap things may appear in this present moment. Every life, in other words, is precious and worth preserving if at all feasible.

To actualize anti-suicidal tendencies instead, take your right hand immediately, and supporting it with the weight of your left, use your fingertips to press in and under the ribs on your left (front) side until you feel a strong but pleasant ache and hold for at least 80 seconds or so before releasing slowly. This will activate your spleen chi, which being associated with the earth element is responsible for maintaining your energetic connection with the planet and hence your presence on or near to its surface.

Then, placing the tip of your forefinger in the dead centre of your forehead in the small indentation you'll find if you spend a moment feeling about for it just below your front hairline, press firmly but sensitively for about 70 seconds as if gently penetrating the bone and release the pressure in slow-

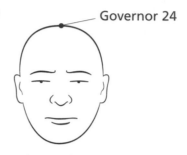

Governor 24

motion so it still feels like you're pressing even after you've stopped. This stimulates the energy centre associated with controlling your own destiny, which is obviously an issue close to your heart right now.

Finally, use that same fingertip to press into the very centre of your breastbone to spark up your heart protector chi which when so sparked fills you with courage, and suggest to yourself as persuasively as you can,

> *'However much of a risk it may be, I choose to stay alive for now'.*

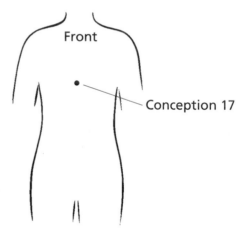

Front

Conception 17

33

LIBERATION

from money worries

I just went in the Land Rover with Mike, trailer in tow, to help him pick up a stove from his friend Arwel who lives on a farm over the other side of the mountain. With Arwel's son, Emir, at the controls of the forklift truck, we manoeuvred the large cubic mass of extremely well-cared-for cast iron neatly onto the trailer and secured it with ropes. Margaret, Arwel's wife, looked on wistfully as if saying goodbye to a dear friend, this stove that had heated hearth and home and enabled the feeding of her family for the past 14 years and was embarrassed to take the hundred quid (approximately 140 euros) Mike offered her in exchange.

While this vignette was being played out by us five actors against a backdrop of rolling hills, pine forests and standing stones, side-lit half savagely by the early morning sun, I was struck by the immense natural humility Arwel displayed in his manner and was all but entranced by the gentle lilt of his voice and kindness that shone in his eyes. Here was a man at one with his world, without airs or pretensions, who knew he was blessed just to be on this land that stretched out luxuriantly beneath the diamond-clear blue winter sky. Yet you could tell he worked hard. The modest but sturdy house, the farmyard, the barns and even the enclosure where the cows were feeding were all immaculately ordered and tidy, yet not obsessively so.

Few words were spoken between us. They are naturally shy people, and yet as often when people are quiet together amidst the grandeur of nature, communication occurs on a different, deeper level, that allows you to feel the very essence of each other, if you're sensitive and empty of internal chit chat enough.

'I can tell you work hard here,' I told Arwel, gesturing about the place with my hand wanting to acknowledge him in some way before taking our leave. 'Ah, well …' said Arwel modestly, not knowing quite what else to say and he looked down at the ground smiling graciously.

As we left, we all shook hands warmly and though having exchanged no more than four sentences, I was touched to the core, by the fine quality of Arwel and his family.

Driving away, Mike explained how Arwel was the grandson of a man who by chance and quirk of fate had invented one of the biggest-selling soft drinks in the world and that Arwel, having inherited his fortune was no less than a 'multi-multimillionaire'; and that the entire sweep of hill and dale we were now looking at as we drove back over the mountain, thousands and thousands of acres of land so beautiful you want to eat it, stretching out as far as the eye can see (without a single pylon in sight), was in fact his.

'Ah well, that's all well and good for Arwel,' I can hear you retort, 'with all that wealth he can afford to be gracious and at one with his world.' But here was a man who would be at one with his world even were he to find himself without money and working as a waiter in a humble taverna on any lesser-known Greek island, offering elephant rides in Cheng Mai or even driving a cab in Manhattan, (for instance).

My point being that when you exercise the humility to surrender to reality, to let yourself be one with your world exactly as you find it, rather than trying to overcome, control and change it, and to do uncomplainingly the work required of you, whatever that might turn out to be, you enter naturally a state of grace wherein all your needs are met. Your inheritance is the Earth and entire known universe; it may not include millions from an inventive late grand-father, but it will include everything you need to support you for the duration of your journey along the 'great thoroughfare' of life — if you, yourself, have the good grace to trust it to so do. (You could call it faith.)

You have to talk to the spirit of the land, whether it be covered in city buildings in all directions or rolling green fields, the mother who sits in the core of the Earth, and say to her, 'Mother, take care of me. Bring me everything I need to support me as I trundle along the great thoroughfare, and in return, I will remember you and come to visit every now and then' — or words to that effect.

It helps to know your bottom line, to know what in fact you need, by writing down all your outgoings in an honest fashion, not kidding yourself by minimizing them. They are only numbers on a page, they won't jump up and poison you. That at least gives her a clue as to which ball park you're playing in, in case she needs to go down to the cash point, which can be well irksome when you're down in the core of the Earth.

The force of the Earth (the material plane) flows through your body as chi from your spleen, the organ associated with the earth element and controls the amount and quality of intake to your person, whether that consists of food, information or material wealth, as well as how you then utilize it to enrich body, mind or pocket. When you worry about money, it weakens your spleen chi. And when your spleen chi is weak, you worry about money.

Conversely, when your spleen chi is strong, money (which after all, is only energy in disguise, hence why we think of it as currency or current) will come to you faster and in greater amounts. And when money flows to you quickly and in great amounts, it strengthens your spleen chi, which is beneficial for your digestion and clarity of mind, thus enabling you to better enjoy the conversation at all those fine dinner parties you'll probably be attending now you've got all that money flowing in.

Spleen 3

To amplify the force of the chi from your spleen in order to increase the amount of wealth that flows your way, look immediately at the top of your feet and especially at the sides where your big toes are. The base of your big toe forms a mound of muscle that sticks out at the side. Just at the point (nearest to you) where that mound begins on the side of your foot where hard flesh meets soft, you will find, if pressing in firmly with your thumb or an improvized poking instrument like the blunt end of a pencil, the source point of the spleen meridian, which, when pressed for approximately 70 seconds on each foot, preferably at around 11am each day (when your spleen meridian is most receptive to stimulation), will encourage the flow of splenetic chi from its source, the Earth.

Do that now. Then sit back as if leaning back into a grand old oak tree (or actually leaning back against a grand old oak tree if you have one to hand) and imagine that instead of leaves, this particular tree sprouts banknotes of the highest denomination and of the most stable currency, which are beginning to fall from the branches and form a huge pile about your feet of millions or even billions (if you think you'll need and can carry them). When the pile is large enough for you – and remember you can come back any time to refresh it – collect it either in your pockets, a large sack or shipping container, depending on size of pile and available imaginary transport facilities, and (see yourself) take it away to be deposited, invested, and dispersed as appropriate.

And don't hold back with the amount on account of misplaced monetary awkwardness. The grand old oak is so flowing with its own spleen chi, it sprouts new leaves quicker than it sheds them. It is, in other words, self-replenishing and ever-bountiful, like the mother who sits at the core of the Earth (the Tao), continually causing things to grow both from the ground as food and from the ground of your very being as (material) wealth.

Do (all) this every day or whenever financially stretched to whatever extent and, like dear Arwel, you'll never need worry about money again ... unless, of course, you want to.

34

LIBERATION

from always being late

In fact, it's impossible for you to be late. You are always where you're meant to be, when you're meant to be there. So whenever you arrive is the exact moment you're meant to be there, and not a second before. Accept that and you're instantly liberated from always being late. Henceforth, you are always on time no matter what.

However, in order to stick to agreements with others (as well as yourself), which after all is the underpinning basis of any organized society (and it's organized societies you depend on for your survival here), you are also required to synchronize your sense of timing with theirs.

For to do otherwise is to rob others, not of their time, because time goes on regardless, but of their smooth running of schedule and hence peace of mind. And the way the law of cause and effect works, when you rob someone of their peace of mind, you rob yourself of it likewise. Specifically, perhaps by having to field phone calls from them on your mobile, during which they accuse you most vociferously of being a flaky good-for-nothing, causing you concern for your reputation and possibly even your livelihood (where the appointment is of a professional nature).

Brian Odgers, my friend and bass player in the original Barefoot Doctor band of the early 90s, a veritable old pro who'd toured the world playing gigs with the world's greats more often than most people use condoms, and who I was sure had been sent to me by the gods to teach me how too to be a pro, would impress upon me by daily repetition, 'If you want to be a pro, turn up on time! That's the first unbreakable rule!' He also taught me that if you make a mistake and fumble a note on stage, do it again straight after (obviously in time with the beat) and the audience will think it was intentional and must have been their ears that went wonky. But that's another issue – scamming – perhaps the subject of a further book.

And it's true, if you don't want to look like a time-divorced, unreliable, spaced out wanker in the eyes of others and risk losing out on opportunities, be on time. This will require a revized relationship with your timepieces, whether wrist-top or mantel-top, whereby you keep a far closer eye on their movements and ear on their ticking in order to check your progress.

Fascinatingly enough, however, most people who are always late suffer from sequence disorientation, omitting to factor in realistically the various sequences involved in getting their person to its agreed destination on time, including, where appropriate, the washing, drying, grooming and dressing sequence, the gathering of relevant belongings sequence, the leaving when you are in good order sequence, the saying goodbye as you leave sequence, and even the time spent travelling sequence.

This entire set of sequences is often dropped completely from the equation, so that if meeting someone an hour's journey away at 8.26, you leave the house after showering in a hurry and forgetting your keys, at 8.32. This can be rectified by writing on a large sheet of paper such reminders as 'shower 6.30, collate belongings 7.00, close down computer and turn our lights 7.12, say bye byes (where appropriate) 7.16, saddle the mule 7.23, on the road 7.26, arrive 8.24, dismount, secure mule and press entry phone 8.26.'

This requires you be honest with the figures and not minimize them to suit your delusional mind. It also requires you coordinate checking timepieces with regular visual revisits to the list, which should be displayed prominently at all times, in order to marry the two as you go along.

Sequence disorientation syndrome (SDS) is often found in those of naturally fluid temperament and arises when spleen chi is too soggy and wet. Your spleen chi, which corresponds to the element of earth, hence operating successfully on the material plane, governs your sense of temperal-spatial awareness.

To be on time from now on, not just according to your own personal time-frame, but also to everyone else's, place your feet together. Slide your left heel along your right instep until it slides off the edge of the heel and into the hollow of your instep. Just at the point that hollow begins is the fire point of the spleen meridian. Now use your thumb (the foot-sliding business was just to help you locate the point) or any improvized prodding instrument with a tip of similar girth to press here firmly (where the hard flesh of the sole meets the soft flesh of the upper foot), angling your thrust towards the centre of the heel. Maintain enough pressure to produce a strong, pointed but pleasant ache that radiates subtly throughout the foot while simultaneously moving your

Spleen 4

thumb (or prodder) in small clockwise circles 'inside' the point, no more than 81 times on each foot. This will heat up your spleen chi, which in turn will dry out the soggy, wet earth and hence yoke you more firmly to reality in no time at all if repeated daily from now on, preferably around 11am when the spleen meridian is most receptive to stimulation.

Meanwhile, discipline your mind by repeating until entranced,

'Time is the best friend I have. I owe my life to it. Without it I would cease to be. The more I honour time by paying it attention, and moving in sync with it, the kinder it is to me and the more flowing and bountiful my life becomes'.

Now would you believe, said he, rubbing left heel against right instep, that days ago Jeb and Mike (who incidentally is always late for everything – reckons it's because he was born at ten months) arranged for us all to go this evening for dinner at some friends of theirs in the nearest town, who want to meet me and I've actually made myself late writing this to you? (Boom boom.)

35

LIBERATION

from fear you'll never find the perfect partner
(including liberation from fear you'll never find a partner at all)

There are many wiser, more experienced and perhaps more cynical (even) than me, who will tell you there is no such thing as a perfect partner.

Well, I disagree on two counts. Firstly, there is no evidence to suggest that whoever you're with at the time isn't actually your perfect partner for the time you're with them, even if the dynamic between you and the quality of your relating does not live up to your expectations. It's all down to what you believe others are sent to you for. If you believe it's to have someone always there who'll be nice to you, not realizing that it's to enrich your soul by teaching you how to give and receive love more freely, whether through pleasure or pain, which will spark off your soul more effectively at the time (and that's something your unconscious mind or maybe destiny chooses without you even knowing), then you're suffering from delusions and will be disappointed. If, on the other hand you accept that where you are is where you are meant to be for your optimum enrichment and that whatever's happening is happening to help you learn how to love more (not less), then whoever you find yourself with is the perfect partner for you at that time. This isn't to say you will never find a different partner who you deem nicer to be with.

You get what you project. You project (unconsciously) from within the aspects of self that most need attention (onto the other) and will have those projections reflected back at you. When, in other words, you have reached such a stage of development that your ego can be said to be fully rounded with no jagged bits jutting out or large cracks gaping, you will project perfection and perfection (whatever that means to you) will be what the other reflects back at you. Until then, you'll often only see the juts and cracks.

Perfection, in other words, is something you only experience in certain moments or sequences of moments, hence a perfect partner is only perfect momentarily. Whether that moment or sequence of moments lasts a second, a day or a lifetime is an entirely different matter, more suited to a book on imponderables such as fate, destiny, astrology, free will, morals, past lives and karmic responsibility, which is all wildly out of this present remit.

Secondly, you are in fact your own perfect partner, and will be for at least as long as you're around. (Yawn, yawn), time for that vibrator or box of tissues again? Not at all. Your primary relationship on this planet, even before your (original) relationship with your mother's womb, is your relationship with your own self. Whether you see that as the relationship that formed between all your dividing cells, the relationship between all your various internal sub-personalities or the relationship between your local self and greater universal self or god (the Tao), it is that which you project out onto anyone with whom you become intimate and then have reflected back at you.

So, in respect of meeting your perfect partner or the one who will always stand agreeably disposed in relation to you and vice versa, you will find that (reflected back at you) either by the one you're with or some other, as soon as you project it. And you'll project it as soon as your ego is complete and you stand agreeably disposed towards yourself all the time. Obviously, if the ego-completion process occurs by degrees over time, so does the process whereby you have that reflected back at you by your partner at the time.

And in respect of ever meeting a partner at all, you'll need to get out more, take more risks, attend to all external aspects that may be inhibiting you, such as hygiene, muscle tone, hair styles, clothes, skin, personality and living conditions, while spending regular time every day working on completing your ego by engaging in activities that stretch your capacity to give and receive love, such as helping others, letting others help you, spending time in groups of like-minded people, such as at yoga, tango, drama, tai chi, spiritual development, rock climbing and cookery groups or even joining a dating agency. Either way, the goal, to meet the perfect partner, must be transformed into developing a well-rounded ego, so you become the perfect partner to yourself, which process can be instigated immediately in the following way.

Situating yourself in a warm, sympathetic environment where you won't be disturbed, take a moderate amount of good quality massage oil, undress, lie down and slowly but purposefully massage from the centre of your chest down the midline of your torso over your pubic bone and onto your genitals and masturbate fantasizing about making love with yourself, for one hour while repeating, '*I now have a perfectly well-rounded ego. I am my perfect partner!*' Then shout out your own name as you come. Kidding. (Kind of.)

In fact, a well-rounded ego, though obviously taking years of real-time experience of both the knocks and rewards of life to achieve, nonetheless arises when your heart chi is balanced (and vice versa), a process which can be instigated immediately by pressing your left thumb firmly into the dead centre of your right armpit and maintaining enough pressure to produce a strong but

Heart 1

Heart 7

pleasant ache, stretch out your right arm to the side at shoulder height and with elbow slightly bent and shoulders completely relaxed, slowly circle it backwards 18 times, then forwards and repeat on the other arm. This is the opening point of the heart meridian, stimulation of which helps clear blockages along the pathway that would otherwise add energetically to an incomplete sense of self.

Next, look at your right palm, and focusing on your little finger, trace an imaginary line dividing it in two along its length from tip to palm and continue the line over that side of your palm until reaching that band of faint, interwoven lines that traverse your wrist horizontally. At this point of intersection, which is known as your 'spirit door', press firmly with the thumb of your left hand until producing a strong but pleasant ache that radiates back along the imaginary line (you just traced), for no more than seventy seconds on each wrist. This is the source point of your heart meridian, stimulation of which induces your heart meridian to draw more energy from its elemental source, fire, the induction of which will calm your spirit enough to afford you a moment of experiencing yourself as a fully-rounded and complete-as-you-are being.

Repetition of these two techniques over a period of 90 days or so along with the following autosuggestion will help reinforce your sense of self and probably draw a (temporarily) perfect partner into your personal orbit, so only practise them diligently if truly ready for that kind of upheaval in your life.

And the autosuggestion is,

'In spite of any doubts I may entertain, I am now with ego complete and no longer in need of validation from others to reinforce that. So being, I now draw the perfect partner (for me for this time) into my personal orbit to engage with in mutual love, respect, admiration, pleasure, fun and adventure!'

36

LIBERATION

from being stuck in a duff job because of the money

You want to live out your life's dream and go full on into the adventure, or you simply want a more satisfying job but feel stuck in the job you currently have because it pays your outgoings which possibly also include supporting any dependants, and it seems you have no choice in the matter and that to do otherwise, to risk all for a dream, would be irresponsible and foolish.

Perhaps it would. But perhaps it would be more irresponsible and foolish not to. For (as you well know) you only get one chance to walk the length of this 'great thoroughfare', in your present body at least, and there are certainly no guarantees you'll ever get another, and at any point along the way you are entitled to choose between minimized risk, reduced personal potential, temporary comfort, a boat left unrocked, apparent stability and security (along with the tendency of these to induce boredom and misery), on the one hand and, on the other, maximized risk, optimized personal potential, temporary discomfort, a boat left rocking, apparent instability and insecurity (along with the tendency of these to induce exhilaration and a bloody good time.)

At the end of it, when you have taken your last step along the way (in your current form) and are piercing the veil ready to step through – an inevitable eventuality that could come at any time – when your life flashes past your eyes, as it's said to do, which of the above would you have rather chosen, do you think? For whichever you imagine would be your preference at that point is a clear indication of which way to go now, unless you don't care if on reaching your moment of death you may have cause for sore regret. (And don't for a moment feel obliged, for the sake of existential bravura or anything as stupid as trying to please me, to plump for the risky way.)

But if you do plump for the risky way and, let's face it, if you don't you should stay in the job you're in, stop complaining and start enjoying it more, which you should do anyway, even if you walk away from it next week, if you actually do plump for the risky way, start now by taking an extremely long and full breath and declaring in full voice (aloud or in your head),

'I am now willing to take a risk and jump into the abyss of not knowing, knowing that reality will reach out and catch me, as it has all the way up till now (and will do so for all my dependants as well). I am now willing to live at my full potential for the rest of my life, in perfect faith that reality will (always) bring me what I need when I need it. I am willing now to let go of temporary comfort to discover permanent comfort within.'

You may wish, if mildly gymnastically as well as ritualistically inclined, to declare all the above while standing on a chair and then shouting,

'I jump into the abyss!'

Then jump off the chair, land (safely) on the floor and say,

'I have now entered a new phase of life, the adventure begins (and I'm a crazy fucker).'

To support this fledgling faith energetically, begin at once by placing hands on hips and pressing for up to 90 seconds into the sides of those ridges of muscle that run down either side of your spine, approximately 2 inches out either side of your spine firmly enough to produce a strong but pleasant ache, in order to release contraction in your kidney region that's been impeding your flow of kidney chi, which impedance has hitherto been causing you fear (of change).

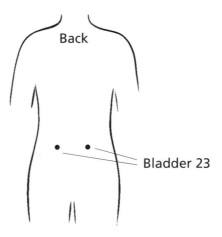

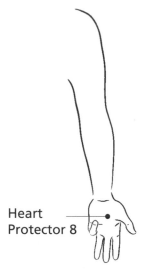

Heart
Protector 8

Then proceed to press the centre of each palm with the thumb of the other hand for up to 70 seconds with enough pressure to produce a strong ache that radiates throughout your palm. These (stigmata) points stimulate your heart protector chi, which, among other things, reinforces your confidence and hence willingness to trust reality to catch you now you've made the jump (off the chair at least).

I'll tell you a funny story about jumping off chairs. When I was still a noisy little kid, unschooled in the ways of the world, my dad, in order to grab a few moments of peace and quiet on the weekends would play a game with me. It was, in fact, my favourite game in all the world. He would stand in silence on a chair in one room (he said) and I would stand in silence on a chair in another, and whoever stood on the chair longer in silence would win. I was very good at it and would stand for many minutes in quiet contemplation. Then, when my dad could (as I believed) no longer manage to remain standing, he would jump off the chair with a theatrical thump that always made me howl with laughter and declare me the winner. That's probably why it was my favourite game – so easy to win. My favourite game, that is, until one day for some reason I'll never fathom, I got off my chair feeling very naughty and crept silently along the wall and round the corner curious to see what my dad looked like standing on a chair, only to find him sitting comfortably on the couch watching TV. And the moral is, never take advice about standing on and jumping off chairs too seriously.

But do take seriously advice to jump into the unknown and let life catch you, because it will if you let it. And in the days and weeks that follow you will notice urges in the belly that will guide you step by step, inner promptings to do this or that, make a phone call, send an e-mail, hand in your notice, walk down the street, turn left or turn right, that will, if you follow them faithfully, lead you swiftly, easily and effortlessly bang into the heart of your own adventure. And I'll be rooting for you. We all will be. *Bonne chance.*

37

LIBERATION

from oppression

People treat you according to what you unconsciously project from within. If you're feeling oppressed by others, someone in particular, a group or the world in general, it is because you're oppressing yourself and projecting the resulting oppressive energy on to them. As soon as you stop oppressing yourself, others will stop oppressing or stop appearing to oppress you.

When you stop oppressing yourself, no matter how oppressive the situation you may currently find yourself in, you will no longer feel oppressed by it. When you begin to allow yourself the limitless internal expansion your spirit yearns for and which is after all your birthright, you will unconsciously project from within the energy of limitless expanse and your external circumstances, including all those that people those circumstances, will automatically begin to reflect that back at you.

This is so even in the most extreme circumstances. I once had the privilege of teaching tai chi to an elderly gentleman (in the true sense of the word) called Israel, a man of exuberant spirit and remarkable wisdom, with the kindest, most joyful smile you've ever seen, who as a boy had managed to stay alive and survive the horrors of being an inmate in a Second World War concentration camp in Poland, watching all his family and many of his young friends die (horribly), without ever having lost the slightest smidgen of his natural ebullience or compassion for others. I asked him how he managed to avoid death. 'I just kept telling myself that inside I was free and I kept moving,' he replied. 'Moving? What do you mean?' His eyes looked off into the distance as if into the past without the slightest twitch of remembered pain and finding words that could only ever inadequately convey what he meant, he said, 'I just kept moving, flowing with the life around me, clinging to what was living, not what was dead, and refused to lose my dignity.'

Picture a wobbly doll with its semi-spherical base. Push it in one direction and it will yield by rolling out of the way using the momentum (of your push) to right itself again. Push it the other way and it will do the same. No matter how hard or from which direction you apply pressure to its surface, it will always yield, roll and right itself again, using your momentum to do so.

In respect of you feeling oppressed, literally pushed against by others, this implies being supple (of mind and body), not resisting the pressure by holding a stiff upper jaw and general posture in a vain attempt to be stronger than the pressure, but to yield to it gracefully instead, while remaining poised around your centre at all times. Maintain a low centre of gravity by letting your mind and energy settle in your lower abdomen and pelvic region. If your centre of gravity is in your upper body and head instead, you'll be unable to yield, roll and right yourself when pressure is applied. You'll be easily toppled to the floor, your dignity (uprightness) lost and forced into an awkward set of manoeuvres in order to regain it (unless, of course, you happen to be a wobbly doll who's been trained how to tumble).

When your centre of gravity is held low, when you allow your mind to be supple and your chi to settle in your belly, you yield with grace to oncoming force – rolling away from the force without losing your dignity. The stronger the force comes at you, the stronger it is repelled by its own momentum, while your inner being remains unscathed and intact. The level of external oppression you feel reflects the limitations you impose on yourself. The more you stop limiting your own self, the less oppressed by others you'll feel. When you have finally managed to stop limiting yourself internally altogether, the impact of outside oppression will no longer impinge on your person at all.

Up till now you've probably thought of having a wobble (in reaction to strong external pressure causing you to lose your balance) in a negative light, like walking a tightrope and falling off – the linear model. But now you can see the wobbles as a positive event, a yielding, a rolling and a righting, a bit of a game you play with life, a dance you do with oncoming pressure – the circular model.

Now you've seen how wobbling in the face of oppression can be a fun thing to do, theoretically, get into training immediately by imbuing yourself with the spirit of the wobbly doll. Stand up, hold your arms, elbows slightly bent, out in front of you at chest height with palms facing you as if holding a fat (vertical) roll of carpet or hugging the trunk of an old oak tree, and with feet shoulder-width apart and firmly planted on the floor, knees bent, thighs firm, upper body loose and relaxed, moving from a low centre of gravity below your navel, circle your torso slowly from the waist in the manner of a Hula Hoop dancer (who happens to be) drawing circles with a pencil (that happens to be) sticking out of the top of your head, on an imaginary ceiling (which happens to be) just a few inches above you, 9 or so times in each direction.

If practised every day, this will not only loosen your waist and strengthen your kidneys, which helps boost your resilience, but will also provide a psychophysical metaphor (a whole army of metaphors, in fact, if you count the carpet, the tree, the Hula Hoop, the pencil and the ceiling, not to mention the confounded wobbly doll) with which to remind yourself to internally yield, roll and right yourself again (and again and again) whenever outside pressure appears to threaten your inner stability or peace.

When you've finished drawing circles on the ceiling, crouch into a little ball, as you'd imagine a child would at times in, say, a concentration camp – contract into the smallest, tightest ball you can manage – and consider all the ways you may be oppressing or limiting yourself right now. Then say,

> *'I now break free of all self-imposed limitations on the full and healthy expression of my energy.'*

Take a deep breath in, mentally gathering together all those limitations into a tight ball in your chest and suddenly, without warning even to yourself, spring into the biggest star jump you've ever done, shouting, *'Haaaaaaaaaah!'* at the top of your voice, visualizing the ball being shot out through your mouth on the waves of sound and disappearing into the distance. (If actual enactment of this sequence is impractical for the time being, simply visualize yourself going through it, including visualizing yourself haaaaaaaaaahing.)

As well as providing a cathartic opportunity and yet another psychophysical metaphor, shouting *'haaaaaaaaah'*, the ancient Taoist heart chi healing sound, will help liberate any stuck or stagnant heart chi, which will in turn help liberate your spirit (spirit is governed by heart chi) from all self-imposed limitation.

Support this by looking at your right palm and tracing an imaginary line dividing your little finger along its length, from tip to base, and continuing that line over that side of your palm until it intersects that band of fine interwoven lines that circle your wrist. Press firmly in with the thumb of your left hand until producing a strong yet pleasant ache that radiates down your little finger for no more than 70 seconds on each wrist, four times a day. This is the source point on your heart meridian and is known as your 'spirit door', stimulation of which will trigger your heart meridian to draw more chi from its source element, fire, which in turn will strengthen your spirit and sense of infinite internal expanse.

Heart 7

(It also happens to be a damn good point to stimulate whenever you're suffering from palpitations, feeling nervous, like say before a crucial meeting, interview, going on stage or when trying unsuccessfully to fall asleep, as it works like a mild sedative within around ten minutes of stimulation.)

Additionally, mantrize (make a mantra of) this,

'I am free to do whatever I choose. I have everything to gain and nothing to lose,'

and in no time at all external conditions will begin to reflect that back at you. Think limitless, think free, think wobbly doll.

38

LIBERATION

from depression

Depression, however much it may somehow comfort you to believe otherwise, is not a force of nature that descends on you from above, from somewhere outside. Depression (literally pushing down) is something you do to yourself – unconsciously, of course. However, once you become conscious of doing it, you then see you have a choice – keep pressing down or stop. If you choose to stop, in time, for like a crumpled pillow it takes a while to plump yourself back up, bit by quantum bit, your depression will lift and you'll have to find a new way to describe yourself as 'depressed' will no longer fit.

Your liver is said to house your inner wild person, the natural self that cried for the breast without worrying about disturbing the neighbours, the one who ran wild roaring with natural delight through the forest at dawn without wondering whether that was making a social faux pas, the self, in other words, before the rules of society had infringed on the full and uninhibited range of behavioural responses you would still display were you able to without getting spanked.

Naturally (or rather unnaturally), your wildness must be contained if you want to live successfully with six billion others on a relatively small area of inhabitable planetary surface. But contained is not the same as pressed down (depressed). Containing that energy means housing it so you can use it at will and the way you use it is to channel it through avenues of expression that will benefit you and those around you – or at least not hinder or harm them. These include channelling it through exercise, work and social interaction.

Your liver chi is what fuels you to go out into the world and play (in the appropriate way), whether that be by exercising your body (all the way from non-competitive 'sports' like, say, yoga, tai chi, dance, rock climbing or even weight training, through to competitive sports like tennis, soccer, American football or whatever takes your fancy), by playing the game of working for a living or for a cause (for it is a game), or by simply going out, having a good old razzle and spray-painting the town red. When your liver chi is (pressed down) flat, you don't feel like playing. Conversely, when you don't play, it flattens your liver chi.

So, the first step is to retrain your self to play. Start by taking up a non-competitive sport and remember how to play with your own body. Join a yoga class, a belly dancing class, a rock climbing class, a dance class or whatever you feel drawn to most. Take a proper walk or run each day. Give yourself an airing. Spend a bit of time each morning before starting the day, stretching out your stiffness and maybe dancing to a jolly tune in your living room. Anything that links your body, mind, energy and will-power will stimulate your liver chi and help reintroduce the natural thrill (of being here).

As your confidence in your ability to link body and mind grows and your liver chi starts flowing again, start experimenting by taking risks at work. Risk intensifying your relationship to those you interact with every day by dropping your mask (more and more often) and communicating from the hip rather than playing the role (of person at work). Reach out. Pay people compliments, ask about their lives, disclose what you're going through (without using it as an excuse to be witnessed wallowing in self pity) and make yourself (more and more often) available to them to do so to you.

As your self-confidence grows in your ability to link body, mind and now the outside world (other people) as well, go even deeper in your experiment and extend your range of interactions to include the social arena. Gently push yourself to say 'yes' to an invitation you previously would have declined (assuming it's not a duff one), hang out with friends at home, in bars, in restaurants (or wherever you like really) and take your living room dance out on public display.

To support your liver chi in supporting you doing all that jolly stuff, stand with your feet at shoulder width, knees bent, pelvis tucked under, spine elongated, especially at the back of your neck, chin slightly tucked under, hands at your sides, breathing evenly, deeply and fluidly, body and mind relaxed and inhaling deeply, make fists. Still inhaling, circle them each slowly in wide synchronized roundhouse punch-like outward trajectories until connecting gently with each other opposite your chest. Turn both palms upwards to face the ceiling by drawing your elbows together, and exhale slowly, deeply and fully making the liver chi healing sound, *'Sshhhhhhhhhh!'* as you draw your pressed together elbows (slowly and gently) into your upper abdomen.

Repeat this cycle no more than 9 times, imagining as you inhale that the in-breath is imbued with playful spiritedness that fills your liver (on the right beneath your ribs) and the wild one within. As you exhale, imagine the *'sshh-hhhhhhhhing'* out-breath transporting all tired, stale chi from your liver and expel it through your mouth.

When you've done, swallow a few drops of Bach Flower remedy of mustard and declare by way of autosuggestion,

> *'I realize now it is I myself who makes me depressed by pressing down my natural playful self, and that it's perfectly OK for me to continue to do so as long as I find it enjoyable, productive and enriching in all ways. I (myself) am also free to choose to let my playful spirit play in the appropriate way for my playful spirit on the day. I hereby terminate my obligation to entertain gloom, self-recrimination, self-hatred, self-pity or any other manifestation of depression. I now liberate myself, step out and play.'*

(Hooray.)

39

LIBERATION

from feeling irritable or angry at others

'At' is the clue here. Irritation arises, like a hot wind, a sirocco up from your liver when your liver chi overheats and you project it (as with a stream of projectile vomit) at either the person who apparently triggered it, but usually at the nearest person available – those you have to live with, those you have to share workspace with, or at complete and utter strangers in line with the new fashion for unpredictable outbursts of public rage, such as road rage, tube (subway) rage, bus rage, air rage, rail rage, probably sea rage (though I haven't yet heard of any instances), and soon, if we don't blow ourselves off the face of the planet from Earth rage before bargain fares for such means of transport become widely available, rocket and space rage too.

Conversely, when you get irritable, angry or give yourself over to bouts of rage, your liver chi overheats. Either way, by maintaining your liver chi at a reasonable 'temperature', the tendency for such bouts to occur is reduced, as is the intensity and duration of bout if one should occur (when someone really pisses you off), hence less time is wasted in subsequent damage limitation exercises, casualty departments of hospitals or police station cells.

So, while there may well be the odd criminal lawyer or couples therapist who, for the sake of business, would rather I didn't spill these particular beans, you might like, if given to such bouts, to avail yourself freely of the following suggestions.

Drink at least 5 deeply-brewed cups of tea made from dried chrysanthemum flowers every day (obtainable from Chinese supermarkets or herbalists, but only use dried flowers, not teabags as the latter are heavily mixed with sugar) as this tends to keep your liver cool. If pre-menstrual, increase to 7 cups, unless you're a guy in which case see a therapist or GP.

Pinch the flesh that grows between your big toe and the next firmly between thumb and forefinger so firmly that you want to shout at yourself and move the flesh 24 or so times in tiny anticlockwise circles This 'sedates' the fire point on your liver meridian, which helps reduce the heat in the wind, enabling you to express your ire, should it be roused, in a more socially appropriate burp of expression rather than the full-scale nuclear spew version, without your feeling deprived or hard done by in any way.

Liver 2

Finally, standing (preferably completely alone and undisturbable) with feet at shoulder width, knees bent, pelvis tucked slightly under, spine elongated, especially at the back of your neck, tongue touching the hard palate on the roof of your mouth, chin slightly tucked in and with shoulders and arms completely relaxed, swing your waist from side to side, turning it about 7 inches in either direction, in such a way as it causes your arms to fly out in front of you, one after the other in a series of strikes to the face of an imaginary (invisible) opponent, one strike with each turn of the waist.

Let each strike fly out with palm open, closing your palm into a loose fist just before your arm reaches full extension, which, if keeping your shoulders and arms soft and relaxed throughout, may produce a whip-like motion with satisfying sound of fingertip(s) gently slapping against palm(s). In some kind of rhythm with your punches, express verbally as well. Some kind of repetitive mantra works best – something along the lines of,

'I hate you, you motherfucker, I'm going to mash you to a pulp'

or something equally as stupid.

As you stand throwing these whip punches and modified verbal tirades into thin air, let your invisible opponent become whomever they want as you rain down your blows on them. You may find them transforming from the person (you think) you're currently angry at, to partner (if not one and the same), to parent, to all manner of imaginary (internalized person), even me (though unlikely), until eventually if you carry on turning that waist enough times they will transform inevitably into your own ornery old self. (After all, there's no one really there but you.) At which point it becomes blatantly obvious that you're a very silly billy.

That's right, you suddenly realize you've been taking yourself far too seriously and as you do, your liver chi cools, and maybe, just maybe, you begin to chuckle, then laugh, then get carried away, laughing till you're roaring so hard you irritate your neighbour, who in a fit of neighbourhood rage, having not yet read this book, breaks down your door and mashes you to a pulp. And it'll serve you damn right, calling me a motherfucker like that.

However, if your ire was too great to still be festering, before it causes you to feel unwell, get up and do the 'Taoist Yell'.

With body arranged in the standing posture as above, with arms by your side, make fists, but instead of throwing punches, inhale deeply, imagining yourself to be gathering up all your anger into a tight round horrible looking ball and with arms slightly bent and shoulders relaxed, slowly raise both fists simultaneously out to the sides, then forward as if describing a huge circle until your two sets of knuckles meet (softly) head to head (as it were) opposite your chest.

Now fling your arms open out to the sides, palms facing forward, like a great performer just before taking a bow, and with throat completely open and relaxed, from the darkest depths of your bowels allow a roar of unprecedented proportions to rise up and escape through your mouth, to the sound of *'Ha!'* (with a soft 'a'). Don't let the sound die away but end abruptly and stand stock still in the aftershock of the sudden (relative – unless you're in this old stone barn with me or in a cave deep in the bowels of the Earth) silence that will inevitably ensue.

If in the city, town or even village, this may be inconvenient to practise often without alerting those close by to your burgeoning madness (and when they come to take you away, they'll find the book open at this page and I'll be done for too), but because you emit only a short sharp burst of noise, if you only do it on special occasions and no more than once a month, which is all it requires, being a very powerful anger (hot liver chi) release, you'll probably get away with your reputation (such that it is) relatively in tact. (They'll believe they imagined it.)

When, having made these or similar practices part of your life and your liver chi is holding at a manageable 'temperature', and you are intending to express your anger directly towards the person you believed triggered it, wait for the passage of at least 9 deep breaths before starting by explaining you feel angry, saying in as relaxed, steady and downwardly modulated a voice as you can, *'I feel angry'* (funnily enough). Then say, *'because, I think, you did bla-de-bla'*. Then say, *'and what I'd like is if you did bla-de-bla'*. Which is all very reasonable and, because you haven't accused them by starting a sentence with 'you', you are less likely to provoke a hostile response, unless, of course, they still haven't read this book (maybe it's that awful neighbour again) and they mash you to a pulp, shouting, '… and you can shove all that communications skills shit up your arse Sonny Jim/Janet, or whatever.'

To preclude the possibility of such contingencies, suggest the following to yourself over and over (at least 6 times for it to penetrate your unconscious properly), while visualizing it too,

'I am now able and willing to express my irritability, anger or rage, constructively, compassionately, authoritatively, politely and effectively, no matter what the issue or with whom.'

40

LIBERATION

from anxiety

Anxiety can be seen as an addiction (see page 124) and can be treated as one. However, as it is hard for observers to monitor in a clinical environment, it is still not popularly treated at rehab centres and the like. Meantime you can treat it yourself, if willing to exercise patient persistence as it is extremely addictive and can take a while to dislodge from your circuitry.

In its chronic form it causes you to expend huge amounts of kidney chi, which would otherwise be used to support your nervous, immune, skeletal, urogenital and reproductive systems along with general vim and vigour, in an ongoing quest to out-think, in pessimistic mode, the (imaginary) future. This makes you far less effective in managing yourself in the present moment and thus far more likely to make mistakes that will give you cause for worry in the manner of any self-fulfilling prophecy. This in turn further weakens your kidney chi causing you to worry more.

Conversely, when you strengthen your kidney chi, you reduce your tendency to worry to the point that, when stable and balanced, you don't worry about anything at all, no matter how dire or scary your circumstances may be.

Anxiety is essentially imaginary fear, which you manufacture at the slightest trigger (usually also imaginary), to stimulate (falsely) your system's flow of adrenalin, which is released in times of true danger to help you physically overcome fear which may otherwise impede your chance of physical survival in any truly life or death situation. Adrenalin is a drug like any other, which causes you momentarily to feel superhuman and is thus highly addictive.

Your adrenal glands sit by your kidneys in your back roughly behind your stomach. According to oriental ways, adrenalin equates to 'kidney fire', the (alchemical) agent that prevents your kidney chi, which corresponds to the water element, from growing too cold thus causing your kidneys to contract and produce anxiety.

When released continually – at times other, of course, than when (you are) in extreme physical danger and sorely afraid for your life or the lives of those you have elected to protect – it gradually weakens your adrenal glands causing them to be able to produce, store and release progressively less adrenalin, so you'll be more likely to respond to instances of real danger in a really crap way.

But more immediately, this adrenalin or kidney fire, becoming weaker and weaker, will, over time, become so weak that it can no longer maintain your kidney chi at a warm enough temperature, at which point it turns to ice or stagnates, causing you to feel extreme anxiety to the point of panic attacks and paranoia, as well as weakening your entire physical system, leaving you prone to a whole list of physical problems (that falls outside the remit of this item to include without boring the pants off you – and me – and turning this into one of those quasi-medical self-help books full of lists).

You manufacture anxiety to produce kidney fire because it's highly addictive (and you love it too much). Your mind then, between the still frames that roll at a rate of 24 frames per second to create the illusion of continuous action so you don't notice it happen, projects that anxiety onto the first plausible 'object' it can find and deftly makes it look (just as any good conjuror could — and there is no more deft conjuror than your own mind) like the object chosen was actually the cause of the anxiety. For example, you receive news that your finances may be endangered and become anxious as a result, or so it appears. When in fact your unconscious mind, which is constantly looking for more excuses to cause your adrenals to secrete their drug, seizes upon the financial issue as a cause for anxiety as a hook to trigger your adrenals. Someone with kidney chi in balance, say someone of stout internal construction, not addicted to adrenalin, faced with the same challenge would be concerned, but not anxious or worried, and would proceed to manage the situation to their best advantage in the circumstances without wasting precious energy.

To instigate the process whereby you stabilize your kidney fire, better to contain it, and strengthen your kidney chi to rid yourself of habitually respond-ing to life anxiously, begin immediately by inspecting your (unclothed) lower leg, specifically in the region of your inside ankle. If the front of that ankle bone points directly towards your big toe and the back points directly towards the back of your leg at the Achilles tendon, trace a line from directly behind your ankle bone up the inside of your leg roughly 1 inch away from the edge of the shinbone and about $1\frac{1}{2}$ inches up from the ankle bone, where you'll find a subtle indentation. Press in here firmly using your thumb or an improvized poking instrument, such as the end of a fine-gauge watercolour brush, with enough intent and persuasion to produce a strong but pleasant ache that radiates up the side and back of your

Kidney 7

calf, for no longer than 80 seconds. Repeat on the other leg, practising every day, preferably around 5pm when both kidney 'fire' and chi are most suscepti-ble to stimulation, for 90 days or whenever feeling particularly anxious.

Next, using thumb and forefinger tip pushed together to form a surface, press into the dead centre of your sacrum and rub briskly but very gently in a side-to-side motion (a centimetre or so in either direction) for no more than 90 seconds to stimulate the production and circulation of kidney fire. This will incidentally also encourage the increase of sexual energy, too much of which will turn you into a right old randy so and so.

To unblock or prevent blocking of stagna-tion or 'icing over' of kidney chi and release or prevent contraction in the kidney region (and hence the anxiety and tendency to worry it causes), place hands on hips and press in where your thumbs land, into the sides of the ridges of muscles (which, if you've been reading sequentially, you should know by heart by now unless half-comatose or suffering amnesia) that run down either side of the spine about 2 inches either side of the

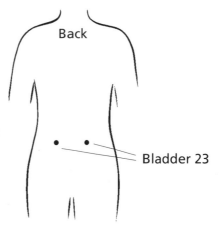

Back

Bladder 23

spine, with enough pressure to produce a strong but pleasant ache that may radiate to the sides, down or into the belly, for no more than 120 seconds.

In the relief of the aftermath, take an extremely long breath or series of breaths and suggest to your self with conviction and feeling,

'Anxiety (and worry) is only a choice I make. I am no longer under any obligation to keep choosing it unless I find it enjoyable and productive overall to do so. I can (and indeed do) choose now instead to respond to (the thought of) all upcoming possible and actual challenges by relaxing, trusting myself to manage and trusting reality to work out for the best (which it invariably does)!'

Or simply say,

'Anxiety and worry be gone now! I relax, let go and allow reality to happen instead'.

Relax, let go and allow (reality to happen instead). That's better.

41

LIBERATION

from feeling like you're missing out

It is impossible for you to miss out on anything. Wherever you are is right at the centre of the action (as far as you're concerned). The more you see that as so, the greater will be your centeredness (and vice versa) and hence the more people will be drawn to you until you become the greatest social magnet the world has ever known. (No one can resist a strong centre – all nature including the human kind, organises itself around the nearest firm centre). The less you see it that way, the more you think the action is happening elsewhere, the less centred you'll be, the less people will be drawn to you and the more you'll run around following others in a desperate and futile hunt for the centre of the action.

Feeling like you're missing out comprises four (overlapping) factors. Dissatisfaction with your present situation, fear that reality has let you down, an incomplete sense of self and a poor recall system.

Situations are only relatively good or bad. If you've just recovered from two broken legs, taking a stroll round the block is like a moment in paradise. If you've just returned from two months trekking the Andes followed by a fortnight lazing in the sun at Punto d'Este, taking a stroll round the block is no big deal and may almost go unnoticed. Your present situation may seem insufficiently glamorous or exciting, but (as far as you know) compared to being dead it's as glamorous and exciting as the finest party full of the most famous Hollywood stars at the height of the season on the largest yacht in St Tropez. Remain with that perspective and anything more than feeling your breath move in and out of your body is a bonus. To feel dissatisfied is not usually so much to do with your situation as it is to do with having deficient spleen chi (however it may appear otherwise at the time). When your spleen chi is strong, you feel satisfied with your present situation, no matter how relatively unsatisfactory it may appear to be. When your spleen chi is weak, you feel dissatisfied no matter how satisfying things appear to be. Conversely, when you feel dissatisfied, it weakens your spleen chi and when you feel satisfied your spleen chi grows stronger.

Feeling complete as you are, having a complete sense of self and the confidence to know you are where you're meant to be, no matter how incomplete your situation may appear; knowing viscerally, in other words, that you are at the heart of the action come what may, arises from having strong heart chi. Feeling like something's missing from your life, even if nothing appears to be, arises from having low heart chi. Conversely, when your life feels complete just as it is, your heart chi grows stronger, and when you feel like you are missing something, your heart chi grows weaker.

Feeling like you're missing something that everyone but you are currently enjoying, apart from being inaccurate and impossible (the chances of you being the only one are nil), arises from having lost your trust in reality to work out for the best. So, if you didn't make it to the ball, you don't stop for one second and think that maybe, just maybe, it's because had you gone you would have hooked up with the very girl (or guy) who would have broken your heart or your cab would have been hijacked by terrorists on the way home – do you? But if you trust reality, you just know that you sitting all alone is probably a blessing and that watching TV is exactly where you're meant to be.

Trusting reality even when you could swear it's just lost its mind, implies being without anxiety, itself a product of strong kidney chi. When your kidney chi is strong, you trust reality no matter how out of control things look. When your kidney chi is weak, you grow anxious and stop trusting reality even when it's all going your way. When you do that, reality gets offended, loses interest in you temporarily to go off and play with someone more up for the ride and starts letting you down (by its absence in your current delusory state), giving you cause (and justification as you see it) to stop trusting it, which in turns makes you anxious thus weakening your kidney chi even more.

You forget that sometimes you'll be the one at the centre of attention, getting all the girls or boys, getting all the laughs and all the invitations to all the right events, and sometimes someone else will. Whatever you want, you'll get it if you wait, as surely as yin becomes yang and yang becomes yin. Forgetting that arises from a lazy recall system, which also arises from low spleen chi (spleen chi controls the efficiency of your recall system).

Thus, to institute the optimum energetic conditions for feeling at the heart of the action at all times, start by examining your right lower leg. Trace a line from your inside ankle up the inside of your leg along the muscle at the edge of your inner shin bone until finding (using great sensitivity of touch) a subtle indentation approximately 3 inches up from the centre of the ankle bone, and use your thumb or an improvized prodding instrument, such as the end of a chopstick, to press with enough gentle force to produce a strong yet pleasant ache that radiates back down to the ankle for no longer that 70 seconds. Then

Spleen 6

repeat on the left leg. This point is one of the most powerful on the spleen meridian, stimulation of which induces spleen chi both to increase satisfaction levels and trigger your recall system. It connects to the kidney meridian (as well as the liver meridian), stimulation of which encourages a lessening of existential fear (of not being in the right place at the right time).

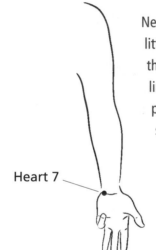

Heart 7

Next, looking at your right palm, trace a line dividing the little finger along its length from tip to base, and continue the line until it intersects that interwoven band of faint lines resembling a bracelet that traverse your wrist. This point is known as your 'spirit door' on the heart meridian, stimulation of which, among many other things, increases your sense of personal completeness (as you are). Press here (in the same manner as above) with enough subtle force to produce an ache that radiates back along your little finger for no more than 70 seconds and repeat on your left wrist.

Now sit comfortably, your back relatively straight without being strained, allow your breathing to settle into a fluid, regulated and relaxed pattern. Close your eyes and let your mind drop into your lower abdomen, there to be centred in what is known as your 'sea of energy', your centre of gravity. Be aware of all the endless action occurring on the planet amongst all the other (six billion or so) people and visualize your centre as the hub of the entire performance (for as you see it, so will it be.) Reinforce this image, by suggesting to yourself often enough for it to become a constant refrain on the breeze that moves your thoughts through your mind,

'I am always in the right place at the right time, doing the right thing with the right result.'

42

LIBERATION

from feeling too easily influenced by others

This arises from not forming a strong enough rapport with your own self to know what it is you want to do at any given moment and, when presented with options that don't suit, feeling without sufficient will to say 'no' for fear of upsetting and alienating others and hence being abandoned.

This occurs whenever there is a disharmony of 'fire and water' or heart and kidney chi, your heart chi being in command of sense of self and all the inner dialogue requisite to reinforce that, while your kidney chi prevents you being ruled by fear and puts you in command of your will to act out (whatever it is you feel like doing).

To support your heart and kidney chi in this respect, begin immediately by curling your hands into fists and, using the edge formed by the curl of your little finger, pound gently, rhythmically and steadily on the centre of your breastbone for approximately 180 seconds while chanting the Taoist heart chi healing sound, *'Haaaaaaaaaah!'* in as deep and resonant a tone as you can comfortably muster.

When you've done (making that noise), stop abruptly, open both arms out to the sides as if preparing to embrace someone you love, then slowly draw them together until the fingertips of both hands touch with palms facing you. Now pull your palms back until resting on the centre of your chest, in an expansive gesture of gathering yourself and cleaving yourself unto your breast, and in that soft and reassuring self-embrace, declare,

'I am now fully at one with myself'

(or something more funky if you can think of it).

Now, using the backs of your hands, rub briskly and firmly in an up-and-down motion (3 or 4 inches either way) on your lower back between waist and lower ribs for up to 200 seconds while keeping your shoulders and arms soft and relaxed and your breathing slow, even and flowing. When you've rubbed to your kidneys' content, stay your hands abruptly and with them resting on your back, allow the heat to penetrate. After some moments of this (still with backs of hands on lower back), breathe in deeply and bend slowly from the hips (either sitting or standing but with legs straight and knees ever so slightly bent) as far as you can comfortably go without straining your back, while chanting in as deep and resonant a tone as you can muster, the Taoist kidney chi healing sound, *'Fffuuuuuuuiiiiiiiii!'* ending the sound abruptly just before running out of breath and draw your upper body up straight while breathing in, ready to start the next cycle. Do this 6 times before placing your hands in your lap, and stating with resolve,

'I choose my own direction. I choose my own direction. And however much I may wobble in reaction to others, my direction remains steady. My direction remains steady.'

43

LIBERATION

from the past (and the future)

Become conscious of your breathing. Let it settle into a rhythmic pattern flowing fluidly in and out, and there, in that almost unnoticeable nanosecond between the inhalation and exhalation, is the heart of the (this) present moment. The breath in your lungs is as much of the past as you can physically hang on to. And when you exhale (it), that's as far into the future as you can possibly (physically) project yourself. Everything outside those parameters is purely in your memory or imagination.

You might immediately like to spend a while just watching your breathing in this manner, thinking 'past' as you breathe in, 'now' in the gap between in-breath and out, and 'future' as you exhale, and may be pleasantly surprised, within no more time than it takes to complete 9 full breath cycles, to find how empowered and exhilarated you feel.

If having read sequentially to this point, and having grown accustomed to my style, you may have already guessed that your lung chi is responsible for maintaining you in the here and now. This is obviously true on the physical as well as metaphysical level in respect of your breathing, which as you know when in a state of cessation for more than a few brief moments will result in your being there and then (a thing of the past, in other words).

When your lung chi is weak, you don't exhale fully, thus clinging to the past (the breath you drew in). Energy (of the past) then accumulates and stagnates in your lungs causing you difficulty in remaining aware of the present moment, and thus missing your life as it goes by mostly unnoticed. When your lung chi is overheated or in excess, as a result of adrenalin (kidney fire) addiction sending flames up into your chest, you tend to spend your time projecting scenarios gathered from past experience into an imaginary future and thus missing your actual life which occurs exclusively in the present moment.

To instigate the process whereby you derive optimum value from each and every moment of your life from now till you die, by remaining fully aware of the quality of 'nowness', begin immediately by balancing your lung energy in the following way.

Looking at your right palm – specifically where the base of your thumb meets that interwoven mass of faint lines that traverse your wrist forming a bracelet effect – and press in with the thumb of your left hand directly over your radial artery at this point. This is known as the source point of your lung meridian. If you place deep pressure upon this point for up to 70 seconds with enough force to produce a strong but pleasant ache that radiates through your wrist and into your thumb, your

Lung 9

lung meridian will draw more chi from its source element, air (traditionally referred to as metal, but that's immaterial to this item). This will help balance your internal energetic environment and help you to remain centred (and hence free of clinging to the past or projecting into the future unduly).

Then inhale deeply and, stretching both arms above your head to open your chest and increase lung capacity, exhale by hissing like a snake, *'Ssssssssss!'* (the Taoist lung chi healing sound), inhaling again as you draw your arms back down, ready to repeat the cycle (up to 9 times), imagining as you do, that the hissing is the sound of a jet-wash, both steam-cleaning and invigorating your lungs from within.

Finally, stand with feet at shoulder width, knees bent, pelvis tucked under, spine elongated, especially at the back of your neck, chin pulled down towards your chest, and palms together in front of your chest in a 'prayer' position. Then say, by way of commanding your mind,

> *'I now release the past fully, and along with it everything (and everyone) I no longer need carry forth into my life'.*

And, taking a deep breath in, thinking of all those qualities (anxiety, doubt, impatience, intolerance, self-limitation, self-recrimination, ill-health, stress and what-have-you), as well as situations you no longer wish to maintain or recreate, and people who would be better served being out of your orbit (for the time being at least), with shoulders relaxed, stretch your arms out to your sides at shoulder height, as if hooked up to a crucifix, and with palms facing out (to each side), breathe out the essence of all you wish to expel (as if) through the centre of the palms of your hands.

Breathe in (again), now turning your palms to face the front, elbows slightly bent so your arms form a wide-open embrace, imagining yourself welcoming the moment and all the good it is capable of bringing your way, and say,

'I now welcome this moment and all the good it brings me, including, health, longevity, peace, love, companionship, wealth, success, joy, fulfilment, excitement, adventure and whatever else I want, in the most compatible form for me at this time.'

(Obviously substitute that for your own 'list' if you'd rather.)

You may wish to repeat this procedure up to 9 times or until you feel you've enacted it with all your heart, soul and mind, and then say, sing or mumble,

'I welcome what's to come,
I let go what's gone,
I'm in the present moment,
having lots of fun.'

Then go out and play.

LIBERATION

from grief

As I mentioned earlier, the last time I was up on Angel Mountain was the day after Ronny Laing died (of a heart attack while winning a game of tennis in St Tropez), 14 August 1989, as I recall, but I haven't had time to press any spleen points to verify. It was, ironically, Jeb's birthday, and we sat in the fields drinking champagne, toasting Jeb's birthday and Ronny's life in the same gulp. (Jeb is a woman, by the way, in case you were wondering all this time). And as the bubbles mingled with the tears (and snot), I remember starting to laugh until consumed by a fit of giggles so extreme I nearly died myself from asphyxiation.

And then, in January 1996, when another dear, life-shaping friend and mentor, Frank Kramer, the man who painstakingly taught me how to breathe through all life's suffering and confusion until it passed (as everything does if you keep breathing long enough), died and the grieving process was sparked up into life once more, I recall, between heaving sobs, giving way to a similar fit of giggles a second time.

Grief weakens your lung chi and causes it to stagnate. When grieving, you tend to go through a phase of not breathing fully, because (as you'll see if referring to the previous item) of your tendency to cling to the past – to the memory of the one you've lost (specifically in this instant by death but also applicable to loss by other less final forms of separation). Giggles, like sobbing, are your body's way of inducing your diaphragm to relax, in order to get your lungs working properly again, and are not (necessarily) a sign, at such times, of an unhinged or macabre mind.

For the first three days after the one or ones you've lost have died, their spirit and energy is still present to some extent in the ether, and it is proper to honour them by spending that privileged time in their (now invisible, yet still tangible unless you're completely numb) presence, during the process of which, if you, in the midst of shock, allow yourself to be fully immersed in the grief, surrendering to all outpourings of emotion, tears and laughter, open yourself to it, you will receive their parting gift to you, the essence of all their received wisdom as it pertains to you in your life. They will talk to you, in other words, as long as you're receptive, and will tell you everything you need to know, in context of your particular dialogue with them hitherto.

After three days or so, their spirit has already gone so far away, you start to lose radio contact. At this point, you are required to let them go, as any vain attempt to cling on your part now will only cause tendrils of gloopy energy to stick to them, slowing them down, and that's a drag when you're trying to cut loose from the Earth plane – or so they tell me. Thereafter, it is common wisdom that it takes approximately two orbits round the sun (two years or eight seasons) for you to heal fully from full-on grief to the extent that you feel complete in your life without their physical presence on the planet.

But the more strongly you can induce your lung chi to flow, the more swiftly, easily and painlessly you will pass through it. To which end, immediately examine your (unclothed) inner arm, specifically in the crease formed when you bend your elbow, in the centre of which are two tendons. Using the thumb (on the hand, unless you have a freewheeling spare thumb) of your other arm, to press here with enough gentle force to produce a semi-paralysing ache for no more than 40 seconds or so, in order to jump start your lung chi. This point must only be stimulated in extreme situations such as grief or during a severe asthma attack, as it is highly potent and, if stimulated willy-nilly, will eventually throw your lung chi into total disarray.

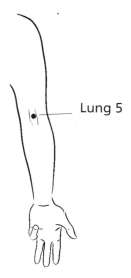

Lung 5

Having people you love and respect deeply pierce the veil and step through to the other side before you, makes the whole idea of dying feel a lot safer. If it's good enough for them to do and not come back, it's good enough for you and me. In actual fact, as any scientist will tell you, energy and, by extension, consciousness, cannot be destroyed, it can only be displaced. And just because you can no longer see them, doesn't mean they're no longer here. Just say,

'There are no ends, no starts, just continuum; sure there are doors, but it's theatre, it's art, and all we do is play our part.'

There now, I've even got you reciting my verse.

45

LIBERATION

from forgetfulness

'Erm ... Errrmm,' (in those immortal words of George W Bush). I've forgotten what I was going to say. (Boom boom.) Which may well be because it's too far to the house to walk there without disrupting my flow and all I have left in the barn to eat are sunflower seeds, of which I've had enough to grow my own internal patch of sunflowers and, consequently, my spleen chi may be weakening a bit.

Your spleen chi is said to govern your recall system, which tends to go on the blink as you age (and your spleen weakens), and which prevents you from accessing pictures, definitions, names, faces, car key location, stash location and all manner of files from your (as far as we know) unlimited memory bank, which itself is said to be governed by your heart chi. So while total or part amnesia arises when heart chi flow is seriously and sometimes permanently disrupted, general forgetfulness, the inability of your recall system to access files or documents, is down to your spleen chi being weak.

So as well as suggesting to yourself, by way of mental command (to yourself), *'I now access files and documents at will, I have perfect recall,'* look at the top of your right foot, specifically at the instep. The base of your big toe forms a fleshy mound on the side of your foot (on which people get bunions), at the beginning of which, the bit nearest you, where the hard skin of the sole meets the soft skin of the upper foot, by pressing with your thumb or an improvised prodding instrument, such as the blunt end of a small crystal, you will find the source point on the spleen meridian. Maintaining sufficient pressure here to produce a strong but pleasant ache while circling the flesh against the bone up to 36 times will induce the spleen meridian to draw more chi from its source element, earth, which in turn will support your recall system. Additionally, place a tiny dab of horseradish on the end of your tongue each morning around 11am (when the spleen meridian is most receptive to stimulation), the very taste of which will trigger a strengthening of chi.

Spleen 3

Spleen chi is also said to govern flesh tone. When your spleen chi is low, your muscle tone will slacken even with toning exercise. When your spleen chi is strong, muscle tone will be preserved even without toning exercise. The same goes for your recall system, which can, in this respect, be likened to a muscle. And, as with muscles, the more you exercise your powers of recall, the more receptive will they be to triggering in the above way. To this end, spend regular time challenging your memory by such games as learning new words, poems, new languages, people's names at cocktail parties (which you should repeat 6 times mentally after hearing for the first time, while attaching the name to face in your mind), musical scales and other such devices for retraining the muscle.

And I was going to say something else ... can't remember what, but in any case, it will help encourage your recall system immeasurably, by giving it the following schmooze or similar,

'My recall system is so damn good, I could eat it!'

46

LIBERATION

from fear of illness

Everyone on this planet, as a living organism, is currently processing all kinds of 'ills', just as they are (simultaneously processing) all kinds of 'wells'. There is nothing much you can do to escape this, even if you enclose yourself in a bubble. It is the way of all form to arise out of nothing (the 'void that is not empty', the Tao), grow to maturity and to return whence it came.

However, as long as the 'wells' are at least fifty-one per cent in the ascendant, you'll survive to thrive another day (and night hopefully), for that is the most you can expect without being greedy or given over to delusions, even though you obviously do all you can to programme your cells to carry you through to a ripe and healthy old age). In fact, say immediately,

'My unconscious mind, is even now reprogramming all the cells in my body for health and longevity. I choose to live hale and hearty, confident and chipper to a ripe old age,'

as autosuggestion along these lines is just what your unconscious mind needs to hear in order to antidote your (mostly unconscious and suppressed) fear of immobility, incontinence, pain and ultimately death.

In turn, reducing that fear frees up all the kidney chi wasted when afraid, which would otherwise be supporting your immune system. Moreover, the more you relax (be in an untroubled state), the more efficiently all your organs work, which has to be a good thing in respect of health and longevity. Conversely, strengthening kidney chi will reduce that fear, as well as help support your immune system.

So, rather than focusing on illness, focus instead on health, for what you focus on grows. Instead of dwelling on your ailments, spend the energy on building up what's working in you. It's the only sensible way to go – to strengthen your immune response, your defensive energy, in other words. Obviously, there are many factors involved outside the scope of this book including getting enough sleep, eating the 'right' food for you (slowly), engaging in regular daily intelligent exercise, comprising internal forms like tai chi, chi gung or yoga and more external, muscle tone and cardiovascular oriented forms, spending time daily outside whenever the weather is fine enough for you, sharing love deeply with people, doing what you love doing with your time as much as possible, sharing human warmth frequently, emptying your bowels and bladder with regularity, enjoying regular uninhibited, healthy, guilt-free sex (protected where applicable), being generous, being receptive, keeping expanding your personal potential by learning new skills and challenging yourself, being like a child, being flexible, being supple, being courageous, being outrageous, loving yourself, thinking kind thoughts of yourself (and others), paying attention to hygiene and grooming, taking frequent vacations and changes of air, taking lots of rest, avoiding allowing resentments to build up, forgiving everyone (especially yourself), not getting too stressed, going easy on all toxic indulgences, not being hard on yourself, avoiding getting into arguments or fights, avoiding random terrorist attacks, earthquakes, sudden sea-level rises and other such eventualities, not insisting on always being right, and always maintaining awareness of your 'higher self', your god, your Tao, your angels or whichever label for the ineffable you most prefer from moment to moment.

But you instigate the process immediately, nonetheless, by placing your hands on your hips and where your thumbs meet your back at the edge of those ridges of muscle that run down either side of your spine, 2 inches or so either side of it, pressing in with enough gentle, sustained force to produce a strong but pleasant ache that radiates into your hips, long enough to feel the contraction there (in your kidneys) begin to release. And, in the aftermath, tell yourself,

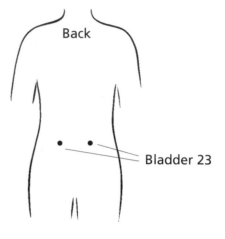

Back

Bladder 23

'My unconscious mind is automatically and instantaneously transforming all fear of illness into kidney chi to make my body stronger now.'

Next, hold both lower legs, just below the knees, so that your fingers are gripping the flesh at the outside of your shins, and your thumbs are behind your knees. Now use your fingertips to squeeze the ridges of muscle (running down directly beside your outer shin bones) just below the knee with enough pressure to produce a strong yet pleasant ache that radiates all the way down the outside of your shins and into your feet. This is approximately the region of your 'three mile' point, the point on your stomach meridian, which, when stimulated, induces your stomach meridian, which is intimately involved with keeping you alive on the planet by strengthening the immune response in the adrenal glands and elsewhere, and hence gives you energy to go an extra three miles. (This point was renamed in honour of Mao Tse Tung's army's 'Long March', on which soldiers would burn the lit end of cigarettes over it to release more energy to keep on marching.)

Stomach 36

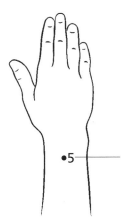

Triple Burner 5

Now examine the upper (down- or hair-covered aspect) of your forearm, $1^1/_2$ inches up from your wrist along the midline (in the direction of your elbow), press in with the free thumb with enough force to produce a strong yet pleasant ache that half-paralyzes your wrist and maintain the pressure for up to 90 seconds before releasing. This is the point on your triple burner meridian, the chi of which is said to govern the good working order of your pituitary gland as well as the healthy movement and distribution of fluids throughout your body, especially your cerebrospinal fluid, which, when stimulated, liberates all the energetic detritus from your outer layer of defensive chi, as well as stimulating your pituitary gland, the master switch of your glandular system.

(So, all in all, it's a good thing to do along with stimulation of the 'three mile' point, on a regular and thorough basis.)

Finally, the 'golden elixir' (of youthfulness, health and longevity) visualization, to provide you with the perfect antidote to sitting around fretting over your health. Sit comfortably, now, with back relatively straight, spine uncrumpled, chin tucked in to lengthen the back of your neck, belly, chest and shoulders relaxed, hands in your lap, tongue touching the roof of your mouth and breathing fluid, deep, even, silent and smooth. Visualize above the crown of your head, the golden elixir of life, as a rich golden fluid, entering through the top of your head, circulating round all the cells of your brain, dropping down through your tongue and throat, into your chest and belly, there to bathe all your vital organs, your sexual organs, and circulating everywhere through your nerves, your bones, your flesh, your fluids, damn it, even your hairstyle, bathing every living cell, making you new and making you well. Say,

'I feel new, I feel new, I feel well, I feel well.'

And, by golly, (if you keep on doing all that) you will be!

47

LIBERATION

from the fear of death (itself)

Picture this: you're a spaceman or spacewoman floating for weeks in undifferentiated bliss, so undifferentiated and blissful that you hardly notice you're floating until, growing imperceptibly larger by the minute, you reach a certain size and state of awareness and suddenly find yourself bumping into hitherto unknown, foreign surfaces. This bumping gives you a sense of other, which in turn gives you a sense of self, and with the passing of a few more weeks, this other becomes a force to be reckoned with, so often are you bumping into it and progressively being forced to accommodate it more and more. Then one day, out of the blue, this other starts to heave, contract and bear down on you as if the entire universe is caving in about your person and you feel yourself being rhythmically forced through an extremely narrow opening that you're sure will crush all the life from you as you pass painfully and awkwardly through, but there seems to be no going back now. And suddenly, before you know what's hit you, you're exposed to the harshness of a new, unfamiliar medium – air, and with it noises, smells, lights and the sudden need to breathe, and as the cold air enters your virgin lungs, you let out a cry.

You then proceed to undergo all kinds of unimaginable challenges, suitable only for those of the greatest courage and ingenuity, challenges, which somehow against all the odds, you manage to overcome. You become increasingly attached to this process as years roll by imperceptibly, and at the point your attachment is as strong as can be, you suddenly feel yourself inexorably pulled towards a veil you've never noticed till now, but which was there all the time, the other side of which is a complete mystery, and before you know what's hit you, you've pierced it, stepped through and you're gone. Returned to that state of undifferentiated bliss, there, forever to float without bumping up against foreign surfaces, and hence without a sense of other or of self or even that of floating. (Perhaps.)

That's what's happened to every person who has ever lived on this planet (as far as we know), and so far not a single one of them has returned. So we have to presume the process is inevitable and in that light it would seem only sensible to stop resisting it, fearing it, denying it and distracting ourselves from it in a million different ways. In fact, it would seem highly intelligent to attempt to reframe it and start to see death as a friend, the best friend perhaps we've ever had.

That means you carry awareness of it with you wherever you go. Whatever you do, however bright the city lights, you train yourself to remember that you're always only one step away from piercing the veil. Instead of resistance and fear, you train yourself to surrender and embrace. And as you grow more successful in your efforts to let go, as you learn to make friends more and more with it, your respect for it grows, your fear for it lessens and you realize that all along it was death itself who was your guardian angel, death who guided you every step of the way and death who will finally draw you through the veil so that you are no more separate from it, at which point, you will feel, indeed you will be, nothing but universal love, for in the end that's all there is. (Others call it 'Tao'.)

So, if you can talk to death and say to it, right now from the bottom of your heart, with the totality of who you are, '*Hello death, I'd like to be friends*' far from making you morbid or sad, it will fill you with such internal power and invincibility that in time, with practice, you'll no longer fear life, no longer fear taking risks and will no longer fear death itself.

But this takes courage, and courage means overriding your fear, and that means removing the stiffness from your heart and easing the grip on your kidneys. A process you can begin immediately by placing a forefinger into the very centre of your breastbone and pressing with intelligence, sensitivity and intent until producing a fine but strong aching sensation that radiates throughout your chest. Maintain this pressure, breathing slowly, deeply, evenly and fluidly, enjoying the subtle sensation of muscular release throughout your chest for a good 90 seconds before saying gently yet firmly to yourself,

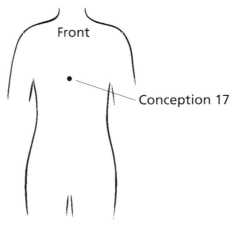

Front

Conception 17

'*I had the courage to be born and to survive so far against all the odds. This same courage prepares me now for an even greater journey into the heart of the unknown. I trust this journey, I trust this journey,*'

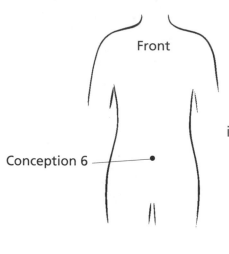

Front

Conception 6

(or words to similar effect).

Now press the fingertips of your dominant hand into your belly 2 inches or so below your navel and keep pressing till you produce a strong (but strangely pleasant) ache that radiates throughout your lower abdomen and into your kidneys at the back. Consciously feel your belly and kidneys relax and, breathing slowly, evenly, deeply and fluidly, while maintaining the pressure, say over and over,

'It's OK to feel afraid as long as I find it enjoyable'

and you'll notice after a while (if you're extremely sensitive) that bit by bit you'll stop feeling afraid, until you hardly feel fear at all any more (more or less).

And then you're flying. (Baby, you're flying.)

48

LIBERATION

from stress

Stress, the undue strain placed on your body and organs by unconsciously gripping your muscles too tight all the time and thus constricting the flow of blood, fluids and energy in your body, impairing your ability to think clearly or optimistically and reducing your effectiveness in every thing you do, is not a disease, other than in the literal sense of having your ease taken away from you. It is simply a habit. But it's a habit that will kill you young if you don't get a grip on releasing that grip and relax (a bit more) immediately.

Start with your buttocks and anus they hide,
and release any gripping all the way up inside.
Feel the expansion as tissue grows soft
all the way from your basement up into your loft.

And as this feeling is spread
from anus to head,
remember softness means living
and stiffness means dead.

But to help you become aware that you're gripping in the first place,
grip even harder from head down to toe,
until you're trembling so much, it starts to show.
Then all of a sudden, you simply let go.

In time you won't even have to do *that*,
You'll be able to relax at the drop of a hat.

Obviously, relaxation is the antidote to stress, and the quickest way to feel that is by practising as above. You can do it all at once or take it section by section, starting by tensing and relaxing your right foot, then your left, your right lower leg, then your left, your right thigh and so on, until reaching everywhere, every extremity and every organ, all the way to the top of your head, and then do it from the head down. After tensing with breath momentarily held, be sure to breathe out fully and let go completely, otherwise you risk a counterproductive build-up of stress instead.

In time, as the ditty says, you'll not need to tense, but will be able to relax at will every single muscle in your body and along with that, your mind, in a trice. The key is in making hitherto unconscious gripping conscious. Once you become aware you're gripping you have a choice: continue to grip, or let go. And while it's perfectly OK for you to keep on gripping to your heart's content, or for as long as you find it enjoyable, in the long run you'll find it altogether much easier on yourself and those around you if you choose the latter. Go on, strike while the iron's hot and say without hesitation,

'I now choose to let go!'

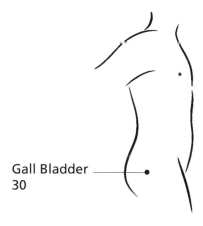

Gall Bladder
30

To support yourself in this process, locate the ball and socket joints at the top of the outside of your thighs by feeling around with your thumbs and without further ado, press in just behind each one where the flesh is thick and keep pressing till you produce an ache that radiates throughout your pelvic floor, including your perineum between your legs and especially your anal sphincter muscles, which when in a state of 'engripment' cause your entire body to strain subtly.

Then release the pressure slowly and with hands on hips press firmly with thumbs into the sides of those ridges of muscles that run down either side of your spine, till producing an ache that radiates throughout your lower back and even into your belly.

Then release slowly and with the fingertips of your right hand grabbing hold of your lower front right hand ribs, and the fingertips of your left hand doing like-wise on the left side, gently prize your ribcage apart until you feel it widen an inch or so and hold it thus,while breathing as deeply, fluidly and evenly as you can for approximately 6 breath cycles.

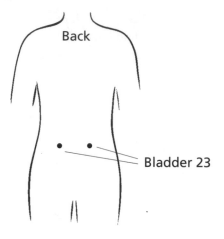

Now, using the little finger edges of your hands curled into loose fists, percuss on your breastbone a drum roll of steady beats for up to 1 minute, moving your fists out over your pectoral muscles until you have percussed on your entire chest, then gradually reduce your tempo until coming to rest in the manner of an engine slowing down.

Finally, press your strongest thumb into the centre of the base of your skull, just beneath the occipital bone (bone at the back of the head), where it is joined by your spine in that soft fleshy depression that reveals itself more clearly when you tilt your head back an inch or two, but which is easier to subsequently press into when you tilt your head forward by the same amount, until producing an ache which radiates throughout your entire skull, main-taining pressure for up to 70 seconds and release slowly.

Raising both hands in front of your face, palms together, slowly separate them one from the other, and draw them together again just as slowly, repeating in the manner of someone playing the concertina in a slow-motion movie. Breathe in each time your hands move apart, and think, *'my space is expanding'*. Breathe out as your hands come together and think, *'all stress be gone!'* Repeat this cycle up to 18 times, enjoying the 'trippy' sensation of chi between your palms, which may feel like water or refined air. When you've done, draw your palms back together to close the circuit and wait while chi starts to flow up your arms and into your chest and down into your belly, where it radiates throughout your body.

If at this point you happen to be living in an ideal world, walk slowly now to where you keep the nearest phone and, having previously done the requisite research, key in the number of a proficient massage therapist and arrange a damn good old 'rub down with a Sporting Life' – as they used to refer to massage in the posh gentlemen's clubs of antiquity – as there's nothing as good for relieving and preventing stress than a properly performed massage by someone who knows what they're doing (and there are many about). (If I ruled the world these would be provided free once a week to everyone on the planet).

49

LIBERATION

from impatience

Come on, hurry up, we haven't got all day.

So, without preamble, let me just say, that impatience, the scourge of post-modern society, arises not because people are dawdling and forming sudden random discussion groups in front of you, blocking your path as you hurry down the street, not because the driver in front insists on stopping on amber at every light and not even because your dream is taking so long to come true, though these (and other examples) may provide the trigger, but because your gall bladder chi is overheating, rising up the gall bladder meridian that runs up behind you, up over your shoulders and into the base of your skull on both sides, energetically overheating your brain and thus disrupting your inner peace (which can only exist when you maintain a cool head, energetically as well as figuratively speaking). Indeed, if sensitive and mindful while suffering such an attack, you may even notice mild discomfort in your upper abdomen, just to the right of centre under the ribs.

You're afraid you'll be late and your schedule will be disrupted. This makes your kidneys contract and squeezes their heat into your liver, which in turn overheats making you irritable. This heat then escapes into your gall bladder meridian, which provides it an overflow channel and in the way that all heat rises, pushes up like a hot wind into your brain.

Gall bladder chi, is normally responsible for maintaining control of logistics as you interact (by the grace of the strength of your liver chi) with the world around you. When overheated you become over-controlling of reality, wanting it to conform to your schedule and as soon as it seems to be letting you down, you become impatient. So, as well as quaffing many drops of Bach Flower remedy of impatiens, grab hold of your left foot, and looking at the gap between

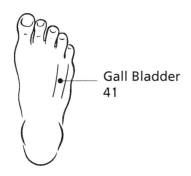

Gall Bladder 41

little toe and next, trace a line along the top of the foot between these toes up to where their bones meet the large bone of the foot. And there in the depression formed, press in firmly with your thumb, using enough gentle force to produce a severe but enjoyable ache that radiates along the outside of the foot, moving your thumb in small anticlockwise circles on the point up to 24 times and then repeat on the right foot. This point is the source point on the gall bladder meridian, which when stimulated, specifically by such anticlockwise pressure-point circling (anticlockwise sedates, clockwise strengthens), will sedate the meridian and reduce the heat, thus helping to normalize your disposition.

Now, to disperse or prevent accumulation of the heat as it rises up through the channel, use the knuckles of both hands to lightly percuss a deft (drum)

213

roll all over the occipital bone at the back of your skull, as well as that part of the back of your neck directly below, paying special attention to the two ridges of muscle either side of the spine. This is a version of a Taoist mind-clearing by 'banging yourself on the head technique', known as 'beating the heavenly drum', which as well as providing an efficacious antidote to fuzzy-headedness and hangover or 'tension' headaches, will also prevent you from being suddenly overwhelmed by the urge to push people out of the way, ram their cars or rob a bank to make your dreams come true. Not to suggest you do it at the time, as this may dishevel your coiffure and cause others to snigger and call you eccentric, but if done every morning in combination with the foot squeeze, will help set up the conditions for patience to prevail in general.

Now stand up and, breathing fluidly and evenly with the entire body relaxed, hands by your sides, tongue touching the roof of your mouth, chin tucked in and back of your neck slightly elongated with feet together and knees bent, jump gently up and down springing from the balls of your feet no more than 81 times. When you come to a stop, don't fall about puffing and panting. Instead remain gathered and standing on the spot allowing your chi to settle in your belly and repeat up to 6 times or at least until you mean it,

'I am imbued with infinite patience, with infinite patience am I imbued. The saints have got nothing on me!'

The more patiently you wait for your dreams to come true, while obviously doing all you can to help them along without attempting to push the flow faster, being actively patient in other words, the quicker they will materialize for you. That's a belief you're free to adopt, for as you believe, so it will be. Just say,

'The more patiently I wait for my dreams to come true, while obviously doing all I can to help them along without attempting to push the flow faster, being actively patient in other words, the quicker they materialize for me.'

Anyway, come on, we're nearly at the end of the book: let's go ...

50

LIBERATION

from your children

(For parents, childcare workers of any kind and potential parents, which probably includes you too somewhere along the line)

As I sit here sequestered behind these sturdy old cold stone walls, I have on the planet, somewhere beyond the mist-shrouded Welsh hills I half see through the window, three sons: Joe, Jake and Michael Angelo or Spike (as in Mike the Spike). At this time of writing, they are 23, 20 and 14 years old respectively, and noble, handsome, sorted dudes the lot of them, who managed by what must have been heavy divine intervention to survive, nay thrive, on my madcap fatherly input from the start and though obviously not without flaw, have all managed to find a state of balance that bodes well for their futures (I hope).

Nonetheless, early one morning in the summer of 1982, when Joe was 3, Jake 1 and Spike was still probably a 70-year-old Hollywood film producer, Tibetan lama, Chicago mob leader or whatever he was in his previous incarnation, I was wandering about the high-mountain desert mesas of New Mexico, as you do, in a state of abject gloom. I'd been there nearly four years training in the various healing arts and was about to return to London to begin my global mission of padding about o'er hill and dale, healing the people and raising their spirits (as any self-respecting barefoot doctor is wont to do). My wife, however, had decided to stay in New Mexico, having hooked up with the weird and wonderful guy with the wispy moustache and piercing gaze, who'd been teaching me 'tai chi combat' as they (you) call it over there in the USA, a euphemism for kicking and punching the crap out of your opponent with alarming precision and dexterity, not to mention chi. His method of instruction was to demonstrate a move and counter move slowly once, then kick and punch the crap out of *me* at full speed till I figured out the move he'd shown me but once and was able to stop him. It was a highly effective way to train when it was possible to avoid concussion or broken limbs in the process, but towards the end of the six-month training when I brought him home for dinner one night and the two of them became enamoured of each other, it became a training in something far deeper, which you can read more about in the item, 'Liberation from the Pain of Envy and Jealousy'.

His overwhelming advantage over me in the field of combat led me to believe there was little point in threatening him manfully to lay off laying my wife or else. In any case, the by-then five-year marriage had degenerated into an all-out non-stop nuclear war and was, as far as I was concerned, irredeemable.

I could deal with that. What I couldn't deal with was leaving Joe and Jake. These guys were my friends. They'd sat in the baby seat on the back of my mountain bike as I sped down mountain tracks, they'd fallen asleep in my arms as I walked round and round the garden reciting acupuncture points and locations. I'd been at their births. I'd even delivered Jake myself. I loved these guys more than anyone or anything I'd ever loved. I'd never even imagined love like that. And now I was going to leave them. (So why not stay in the high mountains of New Mexico, you ask? What, and remain a high-mountain New Mexican new age hippy hiding away from the poisoned troughs and valleys of the global loony-bin for the rest of my life and miss out on all this fun? No thank you very much. No, I really had to get to a global media plug-in point – remember these were deeply pre-internet times – and where better than filthy dirty London (where at least you can get a proper cup of tea, unlike anywhere in the USA, let alone New Mexico, bless it).

At the clinic later that morning (of gloomily wandering the high-mountain mesas and what-have-you), between patients, my teacher looked at me and asked – and this was rare for him, rare in oriental culture altogether, where the whole idea of individual ego takes on a completely different guise to the one it shows up with in our own bloated-chest culture – 'What's wrong, (young Barefoot)?'

On hearing my plight, displaying a depth of compassion and spontaneity quite out of character with his usual inscrutable self, he promptly closed the clinic for the day, stuck the ancient Taoist version of a 'gone fishing' sign on the door and took me to a bar, where we spent the rest of the day downing tequila slammers and discussing the wisdom of non-attachment.

My children are not my children. They are children of the Tao. I am entrusted with their care for as long as fate has it that way and beyond that I have to trust the Tao, the great and natural way of things to keep them safe. I have to trust that when fate has it that we separate, that's how it's meant to be. Furthermore, I have to learn to observe myself and them compassionately but without clinging sentimentally as we go through the process of separation. And though it hurts, I have to trust it is perfect that way. (Substitute 'I' for 'you').

So, it wasn't the end of the world and I went home completely hammered and not a little enlightened. And as fate would have it, my therapist told me to tell wispy-moustache to bugger off, and though incredulous, I did. He, amazingly, backed down. She and I went to couples' counselling, went back to London together and didn't split up for another whole 18 months (of hell), whereafter I was able to see Joe and Jake every weekend (between 10am on Saturday and 5pm on Sunday – the judge assured me I'd find that 'perfectly adequate' – pompous, unfeeling bastard), and did so religiously every weekend till they were old enough to know better.

But my point is, unless you're practising some very twisted, highly effective manipulative ploys on your children, there'll come a time sooner or later when they leave you. Providing you've established a deep enough friendship, based on you having been real with them from the start, honest and respectful, neither bully nor wimpy pushover, kind and protective without being overbearing, encouraging without spoiling, accepting of their flaws and foibles yet not indulgent in their weaknesses, guiding without forcing, and providing you've always given them space to be the total utter arseholes they can be from time to time without damaging their spirits in retaliation, providing, in other words, you've been an enlightened, wise and loving parent (more or less) all along, your friendship will simply grow and grow, no matter where they are in the world.

Obviously there will be times you'll fall out momentarily, just as in any valid friendship. I was an utter arsehole to Jake just the other day, for which I later apologized profusely – these things happen. But there is no reason to believe that your relationship won't bloom and blossom in a series of quantum leaps if you let it. On the other hand, if you've managed to mess things up so badly your child now hates your guts, read the item on liberation from guilt, forgive yourself, make amends as best you can for what you've done and open up a new chapter of communication as soon as you can manage it.

Either way, your kids, hopefully at a sensible age, are going to leave you and it hurts, but once you're through the pain, once you realise that life, the Tao, had them in its arms all the while, that they are not you or an extension of you, but people in their own right, as indeed they always were, a wonderful freedom radiates to every region of your body and you almost feel compelled to yell, 'I'm free!'

Not that you stop caring. You love them and care for them more with every breath you take. It's simply that you've liberated yourself from the delusion that you're responsible for every move they make. *They* are now.

Now it would be really daft to start talking about which point to press or which sound to make to liberate you from your children. I mean, you could always press a confrontation to the point of no return and shout loudly, 'Get out and don't come back!' but I'm sure that's not what you had in mind.

Identity confusion, believing your kids to be an extension of you arises from heart chi deficiency (heart chi provides you with a full sense of self and hence others).

Over-control, trying to remain in control of your children's destiny forever, arises from overheated gall bladder chi, itself arising from overheated liver chi, that arising from over-contracted kidney chi, which occurs when fundamentally, you're full of fear.

Inability to let go in general, arises when your large intestine chi is weak or blocked (as with the ability to let go of waste matter from your bowels).

So there's nothing to stop you using your knuckles for a few moments of percussive insanity, to gently rap a fast, steady drum roll all over the back of your skull, especially either side of your spine just below the occipital bone at the back, in order to disperse hot gall bladder chi that tends to get stuck in that region.

Moreover, if you simultaneously breathe out making the liver chi healing sound, *'Shhhhhhhhh!'* while visualizing your liver cooling down beneath your right hand ribs, it won't have any adverse effects.

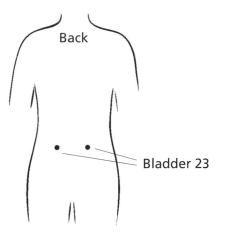

Back

Bladder 23

Nor will pressing your thumbs into the points 2 inches either side of your spine just above waist height to reduce contraction in your kidney region and help support your liver.

And finally, you can never go wrong rubbing your entire belly with palms in a clockwise circle up to 81 times to strengthen and unblock large intestine chi, while suggesting to yourself,

'I am not my children's thoughts and feelings. I am not even my own thoughts and feelings. I simply am a child of the world doing the best I can. We are all looked after here, as soon as we realize we are.'

And any time you find yourself worrying about your children, be aware that this projects negative, harmful thought rays (destructive chi) in their direction.

Instead, visualize them surrounded in an impenetrable aura of protective white light. It works. This obviously applies to people other than your own children. In fact, it is a valid and worthy exercise to spend a moment imagining that every living creature is one of your children. It helps you love them all more. (Go on, have a go.)

51

LIBERATION

from your parents

It wasn't till my early 20s in therapy with RD Laing that I even noticed there was a difference between my parents' thoughts and my own. I mean I'd always known I had my own thoughts separate from theirs (and I think of them individually), but had never actually acknowledged it. To actually examine the difference between what I believed and what had been inculcated into my wiring by 20-odd years of parental propaganda, the main tenet of which was that my parents are always right. Now obviously they've been right about many things, but there's no way they or anyone else's parents could possibly be right about absolutely everything. I know for a fact, in fact, they weren't.

I can say that now – easily. But that first time sitting in Ronnie's consultation room, with him giving me that quizzical little look of his as I stumbled on the realization, I could hardly spit the words out. It felt like out-and-out sacrilege. What, my dad wrong? You mean I'm free to form my own independent beliefs about life, on my own? No authority figure except me? You mean I'm in charge here?

And, of course, it didn't stop there. I'm still sifting through, sorting what's his and what's mine. In retrospect, my mum actually does seem to have been right with just about everything she's ever taught me even about being right about everything, and consequently the sifting process has been easier with her.

Along with the realization that your parent or parents are fallible comes the realization that they're human, were once babies and don't really have any more of a clue about life in the grander sense than you or anyone else. And this is difficult. It's painful and squirmy to see your hitherto perfect parents as vulnerable fucked up people just like you. It's a lot to take on, except in those rare cases where parents were enlightened enough to be willing to be real with you as opposed to right, and where you already knew them as they were and had learned to accept (and forgive) them from the start. Unfortunately, many parents pretend with their kids. They take on the role of parents in place of simply discharging their parental duties while being themselves (as in the children they were before you or your siblings came along). They get lost in the role. You, by effect, take on the role of child and get lost playing that role, instead of simply discharging your filial duties while continuing to be the person you are around your friends and people who treat you for who you are and not some little kid.

But there comes a point, usually around the time you start earning your own living and are no longer so dependent for your physical survival on your parents or their set-up, that you begin the process of differentiation – a process which continues all the way till you die and maybe even beyond, who knows. A point where you stop and say, 'Hey, wait a minute. I'm not my mother's thoughts, beliefs or feelings. I'm not my father's thoughts, beliefs or feelings. Hell, I'm not even my own thoughts, beliefs or feelings. I just am. And as I am, I'm free to choose to think, believe and feel whatever I want, from minute to minute, as I go along!'

And you've got to let go of seeking their approval too. Of course, we all want and are, consciously or unconsciously, at least partly driven by our desire to gain our parents' approval. It starts as a baby. If you don't learn to perform the basic tasks of eating, digesting and eliminating, which are invariably taught you by stick and carrot methods, you quickly end up as just another infant mortality statistic. So, it's programmed in from a young age to help ensure your survival. But at a certain point when your survival depends on your ability to think for yourself in an original way, you have to switch tactics from trying to gain their approval for your actions to trying to gain your own, which after all is far more important.

But the first stage is recognizing the difference between you and them. This is made much easier by stimulating your heart chi, on account of the latter being responsible for a clearly defined sense of self. All identity crises indicate weak or ill-defined heart chi and, by the same token, whenever your heart chi is weak or ill-defined, you are more prone to identity crises, along with which you'll find it more difficult to know what you think, feel or believe about anything.

Personally, if I ruled the world, I'd have two years of therapy mandatory for everyone at school-leaving age, a little like doing compulsory military service or having to be a monk as they make all the boys do in Thailand. This would be specifically to help everyone through that particular passage into adulthood which necessarily includes defining the appropriate boundaries between you and your parents, and to help you become your own parent and your own person, there in the front line and giving it some, if you'll excuse me waxing so gung ho.

However, if therapy is anathema to you, or hard to come by because of expense, free time or location, you can help the process immeasurably by pounding roundly (but intelligently so as not to break any bones or dislodge any ribs) on the centre of your breastbone with (the little finger edges of) your fists while chanting the heart chi healing sound, *'Haaaaaaaaaah!'* for up to 9 breaths' worth. This will shake up

your heart chi and help dislodge any stuck energy that may be causing blurring of boundaries in terms of your sense of self.

Now settle it by pressing firmly into your wrist bracelet just beneath the palm on the ulna (little finger) side. This is the source point on your heart meridian and is known as your 'spirit door'. Stimulating it encourages your heart meridian to draw more chi from its source element, fire and generally increases your sense of self, complete with personal boundaries, quirks, foibles and that *je ne sais quoi* they all say you have. Press with enough gentle force for about 40 seconds to cause a strong but pleasant ache to radiate the length of your little finger and release slowly, while affirming,

Heart 7

'I am my own person. I automatically retain all valuable beliefs while eliminating the rest. I am my own wise, loving parent and I have my utter approval. In fact, I'm altogether so fantastic I don't know what to do next!'

(You could always read the following.)

52

LIBERATION

from time

There's no time to talk about that now, there's simply no time. And therein lies the clue to liberation from the clutches of time.

And now from the stone confines of this mountainside barn, confines which though not sad to leave in but a few hours, I will no doubt severely miss (that's the odd thing about liberation – you often tend to suffer withdrawal symptoms from whatever or whoever you've been liberated), I am about to attempt the impossible: an explanation of time (from the metaphysical standpoint).

Firstly, there is no time, there is merely movement through space on (or in close proximity, when underground, or in a plane or rocket, to) the surface of a planet spinning round the nearest star at 19 miles per second. Owing to this motion, and on account of the planet's axial tilt catching the heat from that star in varying amounts according to the planet's position relative to that star at any point in its (the planet's) trajectory, local weather systems change according to some sort of more or less predictable pattern and nature responds by either retreating or blooming depending on the amount of heat available. Moreover, on account of the planet rotating on its own axis at 1000 miles per hour, approximately half the time you spend on its surface will be away from the light of that star, and the other in its full glare (cloud formations and movement patterns permitting), though the ratio of dark to light will also vary according to axial tilt shifting through the various phases of orbit.

Thus, our years, seasons, days and nights (and hence, weeks and months) are merely constructs employed as measuring devices to enable us to maintain comprehensible work-a-day schedules. And while during the course of this motion (circular motion as opposed to linear, implying incremental aging), your body gradually surrenders to entropy, as does any moving mass, you never feel any different, (older, in other words).

We constructed our model of linear time back in the days when mythologies were still up for grabs, in order, I would presume, to prevent everything occurring simultaneously. However, when you position yourself internally, so that your mind is centred in your belly, your chest is relaxed and your skull cool and empty, and you observe the procession of unfolding events that comprize the story of your life, it becomes immediately evident that you are in line with the circular motion of the planet in space, at the hub of a great wheel, whose rim is comprized of the moments of your life.

This isn't an intellectual myth-driven concept, it's a meditation suggestion, for as I disclaimed, this item is all but impossible to write successfully.

Nonetheless, the facility for continuous, uninterrupted present-moment centeredness, necessary for your liberation from the clutches of time, occurs by grace of your heart chi, that which governs your greater sense of (universal) self or spirit. In respect of which, immediately examine your right palm and trace an imaginary line that divides the length of your little finger from tip to

Heart 7

base. Continue the line over that side of your palm until it intersects that band of faint interwoven lines that criss-cross the underside of your wrist, at which point, press in with your left thumb for up to 90 seconds, with enough gentle force to produce a strong yet pleasant ache that radiates back along your little finger, release slowly and repeat on the left wrist. This is the source point on your heart meridian, stimulation of which encourages your heart meridian to draw more chi from its source element, fire, and thus less from the 'world of the ten thousand things'. In other words, your mind, which is said to be governed by your heart chi, is less drawn to worldly distractions and is more able to draw its sustenance from within, enabling you to see things in their circularity rather than, or as well as, part of a linear sequence. In other words, pressing this point may help you contemplate time in a new light. Or it may just induce deep feelings of relaxation, so you stop caring about time (and hey presto, you're liberated).

In any case, we have constructed this illusion we call time, we've breathed life into it generation after generation. And for that it is worthy of honour, in the same way we honour the myth of Father Christmas.

But I can't sit around here all day discussing this. Firstly, I'm not nearly sufficiently clever or erudite to do anything more than make it even more confusing, and secondly,

I simply haven't got time. The book's nearly finished and is going at such a pace, if I don't move on to the next item, I may get stuck between these pages and never escape from under its covers, be caught in a time warp in other words, and that just wouldn't do. I've still far too much mischief to make in the 'world of the ten thousand things'.

53

LIBERATION

from suffering

Suffering is a choice you make.

No, that isn't intended as callous. Hear me out.

I could sit here cold and alone with no mobile signal beneath the low ceiling of the cloudy grey sky and the dry ice-like mist obscuring my view, suffering if I choose. Or I can, like the six wild horses sleeping contentedly on their feet, as it were, outside my window, surrender to what is, stop resisting, stoke up the stove and choose to love it, or at least love taking pride in the fact that I've not run away back to the city, or better still to a sun-drenched beach (oh yes!) before completing the cycle like some urban girl's blouse.

I, like you, can dwell on the pain, or dwell on the pleasure. Every moment has its fair share of potential tragedy as well as its fair share of potential triumph. Focus on the tragedy and it will grow until it overtakes the moment and you're suffering (again). Focus on the triumph and it will grow, until it overtakes the moment and you're liberated from suffering. This holds true, no matter how extreme the circumstances, providing you don't panic so much you can't see the wood for the trees.

Suffering in the abstract sense has been passed down (mostly unconsciously) from generation to generation and adopted (mostly unquestioningly) as a habitual response (to life). Adopted (mostly unconsciously) as a perceived obligation, as if to perpetuate it would somehow alleviate the suffering of those who have gone before. But no matter how much your ancestors (and especially parents) may have suffered in their lives, no amount of suffering will take that away. On the contrary, suffering only adds to suffering, while triumph inspires triumph.

But the time has now (surely) come, for us to choose to break the mould and drop suffering from our agendas. And as we do, as you do, one by one, faster and faster, others will be inspired to do so too and then maybe, just maybe, with suffering off the agenda, we, as a species, will finally learn to leave each other be in peace.

Or maybe we won't, but either way, it behoves you personally to begin the process of self-liberation from suffering immediately, so that you may more quickly begin to inspire those in your circle and those you meet, to do likewise, until bit by bit a new suffering-free paradigm emerges in the world (of people), at which point, I for one, work done and mission accomplished, will stretch out on a nice warm beach, fall promptly asleep in the sun and pretend none of this really happened. Don't know about you.

The chi in your body that protects you from the pain of suffering, is that of your 'heart protector'. Essentially, whenever your heart protector chi is weak, you suffer, even if in a penthouse suite of a 6-star hotel, looking out at the sunset without a care in the world. But when your heart protector chi is strong, you will not suffer and indeed will triumph, were you even shivering, cold, tired, wearing brown shoes with navy trousers, having a bad hair day, riddled with pain, with nowhere to sleep tonight, no money in your pocket, with night falling and it just starts to rain. You'd just laugh and shrug it off. It (the chi) would have to be pretty damn strong for that, mind you. (But you get my point.)

So saying, take hold of your wrist and examine its underside, where no more than two inches up from those interwoven fine lines that form a bracelet effect where palm meets arm, between the two tendons that run together up the midline of your forearm, is a point, which if pressed by thumb-tip with enough gentle force to produce a strong but pleasant ache that radiates back into and throughout your palm, half-paralysing in its effect, for no more than 70 seconds on each wrist, will activate the production and circulation of enough heart protector chi to make you skip merrily through the nastiest storm.

Heart Protector 6

Having done so, reinforce the effect, by declaring with contained gusto and serious intent,

'I now declare an end to suffering in my life. I am no longer obliged to suffer for anyone else's sake or my own. Of course, it's perfectly fine to continue to suffer for as long as I find it enjoyable, however, the more I suffer, the more others suffer with me. The more I let go of suffering as a

habitual (bogus) response to life, the more peace (and pleasure) prevail. May peace and pleasure prevail now (for me and anyone on the planet who wants it).'

An end to suffering ... now.

54

LIBERATION

from this book never coming to an end and winding up being too heavy to carry around

So here I am, as if all of a sudden, finally on the 12.30 out of Swansea heading east to the hills and valleys of London, there among the concrete, granite, brick, glass, pollution and noise to re-enter the affray and general mayhem of the world at large. Liberated from the sobering solitude of the old stone barn on its wild and windy mountainside, just in time to miss the full effects of the change of weather that was beginning to force damp and cold to bite my bones through the gaps in the old Land Rover even as Mike drove me to the station.

Out of isolation and back to a thousand and eight text messages, voice mails, e-mails and demands on my time from a million (and four) different quarters at once, but desirous before I exit this particular dialogue with you, to leave you with my love and to thank you for being kind enough to chum me along while I chatted away at you like a crazy (short-term, as well as often nearly short-circuited) hermit.

And to congratulate you for joining the hallowed ranks of Simon Bolivar, Che Guevara and all the other great liberators of history. For by displaying the courage to begin your own process of self-liberation, you'll inspire others to begin it too, and before you know it you'll have been responsible for liberating the entire world.

At which point, even the Buddha (who according to esoteric hearsay, though having been desperate to make it back to the 'Pure Land' for many centuries now, has instead, on compassionate grounds, been hanging around in the ether until every single one of us is finally free of suffering), will clap his hands in glee and shout, 'Free at last, free at last, lordy, lordy, I'm free at last', or more Buddha-flavoured words to that effect, and a thousand angels drinking celebration cocktails will stop to dance a jig around their handbags and sing 'halleluiah'.

And may the sound of their voices follow you wherever you go, comfort you every step of the way and remind you to stay free, just as the voices of these two angels from Angel Mountain, Jeb and Mike have been doing for me.

And now the time to say 'ta ta' is here
But be not sad, nor filled with fear.
There are no ends, no starts
Just continuum.
Sure there are doors,
But it's theatre, it's art,
And all you do is play your part.
All you do is play your part.

And you just played your part (of being 'reader')
with grace and aplomb.
You've been a wonderful audience so don't go changing now,
('cos you're the bom!).

Till next time. (Bless you.)

Barefoot Doctor, Paddington Station, London 2002

Return of the Urban Warrior
High-Speed Spirituality for People on the Run

The Barefoot Doctor

Barefoot Doctor takes you on a high-speed 'spiritual' trip – with potent doses of humour and demystified Taoist philosophy – containing (almost) everything you need to know to excel in the fast furious twenty first century without cracking up. Includes:

- Advanced Taoist meditation and self-healing techniques for beginners and old hands alike
- Contemporary urban Taoist life skills to help you 'spiritualize' even the dullest moments and be the slickest operator on the block
- The ancient Taoist 'warrior wisdom' programme for peace, prosperity and peak performance installed into your circuitry simply through reading (this text).

Barefoot Doctor, healer and media presence, author of Handbook for the Urban Warrior and teacher of Taoist self-help techniques, has been practising for over two decades, specializing in personal liberation. The original barefoot doctors travelled the ancient Orient, healing people and lifting their spirits. This is the twenty-first century urban version.

Make
www.elementbooks.co.uk
your online sanctuary

Get online information, inspiration and
guidance to help you on the path to physical
and spiritual well-being. Drawing on the integrity
and vision of our authors and titles, and with
health advice, articles, astrology, tarot, a
meditation zone, author interviews and events
listings, www.elementbooks.co.uk is a great
alternative to help create space and peace
in our lives.

So if you've always wondered about practising
yoga, following an allergy-free diet, using the
tarot or getting a life coach, we can point you
in the right direction.

thorsons
element